A FIELD GUIDE TO

NORTHFIELD

ISBN 978-0-939394-18-0

Published in the United States by Black Willow Press.
www.blackwillowpress.com

Book design and illustrations by Mark F. Heiman

A FIELD GUIDE TO
NORTHFIELD

NANCY SOTH

BLACK
WILLOW
PRESS

To Molly Daniels Ramanujan

CONTENTS

INTRODUCTION

THIS IS MY SECOND BOOK ABOUT NORTHFIELD. THE FIRST ONE was called *Fantasy Northfield*, and in this one I've tried to have a little less fantasy, but it's hard to do. I've tried to write more about real people, but I made up some. Because I thought a tour of Northfield might be vital, I made up Estelle and made up a tour. Last September, just before Defeat of Jesse James Days, I thought I saw a real tour guide. It was 85 degrees but I had to go down to mail a letter at the bottom of the library hill and there were two excited little boys and their dad having great fun with the big rock deep sea sculpture. They were accompanied by another interesting figure in a curious costume, and I thought that perhaps in advance of Jesse James Days we had a tour guide, costumed, but perhaps not skillfully. Soon the boys and their dad left, and the costumed tour guide was left standing all alone. I asked him about his tour guide business, but soon found out that he had a bit of an English accent and that he had just come from a Revolutionary War reenactment and decided to keep his wool costume on. I thanked him, told him it was a hot day, and shook his hand, even though he was probably on the enemy's side. Walking across the street to the mailbox I saw another dad and his college-age daughter having lunch on the porch at Chapati's, and felt it was my duty to keep them informed. When I asked them if they knew what the guy across the street was doing, they had decided! It was a history professor!

This was so good that I had to tell Marie Gery, (totally real), who wrote: "The story is too good—and too true. Perhaps it would help the local image if college professors did dress the part. This, however, would call for a great deal of creative thinking for folks in quantum physics or neuroscience. Philosophers could choose their faves and dress accordingly. English profs, ditto. How could it be dreadful to dress as Elizabeth Bennett or Isabel Allende? Unless, of course, one was male. In advance of J2 Daze—Lord only knows what and who will arrive. Do keep me informed about your forays into the Land That Time Forgot otherwise known as Division Street."

Later, Jane McDonnell suggested that physicists could dress as the Higgs Boson—very shy, but also acting like molasses. Jane had some close family connections with the Higgs Boson.

I didn't really write this book. I kept my ears open and became a spy whom friends could no longer trust. Otherwise, I usually just copied everything from MPR, the *Northfield News* or Griff Wigley's *Locally Grown*, or the *New York Times*, *Minneapolis Star Tribune*, *Carletonian*, *St. Olaf Magazine*, or Google and connected them all by stream-of-consciousness paragraphs which I discovered in 1976 and call Kitten on the Keys. Back then it was a sort of a demonic typing on paper, throwing each sheet on the ground as a mad pianist. Now it's just clicking.

Also, I had some leftover Police Logs which appeared after my last book was published, so I've put them in the same old place, as a testament to what's now been lost, either in the life of crime or the life of journalism.

Confessions: Okay, I also made up one downtown business. I made it up because it's something a lot of us older people need, but the Pantorium was once real. I guess I really made up a lot of things, but most of the people other than Estelle are real. I wanted this book to talk about Northfield people, wanting to honor them, but can you believe this? I soon found out that not everyone wants publicity. Stop me before I make up everything! I just wanted to introduce our great characters, remember that they once lived here. I wanted them to live permanently in the book, even though it's just a paperback. I wanted to remember our Northfield children, even if they no longer live here. They still continue to gather together as Northfielders when needed, perhaps even if it's only on Facebook, in times of Northfield sorrows, Northfield victories, and Northfield fun.

My greatest shame is that once again I don't know enough Tyvek Towners or West Siders to write about. I'm not a person who believes you can have too many friends, but I wrote too much about my neighborhood once again. I did take some walks and kept my eyes and ears open walking to the Ole Store Café or St. Olaf and if I've learned anything in writing this book, it's that it pays to start getting curious with strangers.

All the great friends and the many clever strangers who wrote most of this book are captured forever at the end of this book on the last page.

Nancy Britton Soth
nancy.soth@gmail.com
2014

WHO ARE THESE PEOPLE?

Oh, you must be from Tyvek Town, named for that pink or white stuff that goes around new houses. We're excited about your coming, but you're making it impossible for us to hike our town in a day without panting. Northfield is inflating. But you may not know yet about Northfield exceptionalism. Stop the Urbanity! We used to call anything south of Seventh Street "the suburbs," then compromised and called anything south of Woodley "SoWo."

LET US INTRODUCE YOU

Welcome! We might not have a flag on our Perkins, although in some towns the Perkins flag flew over them as if it were an aircraft carrier. (However, give that big flag some respect. It can also fly at half-mast.) Still, you'll feel proud when you see those four flying American flags at the service station on Division and Woodley. No Perkins flag, but we had Puppy Head Start (for puppies from ten weeks to five months),

---

I'm so Northfield I actually got lost somewhere south of Sibley in all the new developments. — Jonathan Shepard

Puppy First Aid, lessons in Puppy Massage and rain barrel workshops. Other dogs got foster homes and Adopted Dogs had their own reunions at Prairie's Edge Humane Society.

You're going to love it. Now, Northfield has no problems, only issues. All our old problems were simply issuematic. (And the *Minneapolis Star Tribune* reported that even eggplants have issues.) God had blessed us with an abundant shower of retired Lutheran ministers, emerging and submerging artists, socialist socialites, undercover vegans, retrosexuals, and promising poets.

WE'RE NOT PIONEERS BUT WE'VE BEEN HERE LONGER THAN YOU

We cherish our individualism; even our watermelons are personal. As for us, we're *outré* grannies, not content to remain a novelty, who choose to live metaphorically. And many of us were terminally quaint, still living with many secrets hidden in our underwear drawer. Nevertheless, we've made some progress. Our Wisconsin mothers ordered their toilet paper delivered from Gimbels, too embarrassed to buy it in the grocery store. We knew Snowden when he was just a cute little bear that Target advertised at Christmas.

According to a letter from Arthur Paul David White, our favorite local correspondent to the *Northfield News:* "Through Northfield, the entire universe will be transformed. Stay tuned." When Art White ran for mayor we all carried signs saying: "Art for Art's Sake." However, we'll just be a little more modest than Art and appreciate the smaller things.

MAKING SENSE OF NORTHFIELD USING THREE OF THEM

Northfield is fragrant: bread baking in restaurants in the morning, the good smell of frying by the Tavern in the afternoon, tempting anyone on a low fat diet, the Chinese spices from the Mandarin Garden, not too far away. College students, coming back for reunion, would say how they had missed the Northfield smell, not able to name exactly what it was. Even the fragrance of manure in the fields held promise. And then there

I'm so Northfield the smell of manure makes me homesick. — CGF

was Malt-o-Meal enveloping the town with its chocolate and cinnamon. Megan Wille, a Northfield student graduation speaker, loved the Apple Cinnamon Toastee-o's from Malt-O-Meal, a scent that would occasionally waft over the high school—and when it did, "you have to smile." And Helen Woehrlin had a special talent for Malt-O-Meal diagnosis. There was vanilla, cinnamon, chocolate, and even a toasty "burning" smell.

Michael Groeneman, a recent Carleton graduate, confessed that "I think the greatest of my teachers was the Malt-O-Meal factory. It taught me that even in challenging times, there is a sweetness to be had in the world if you just breathe deeply and take it all in."

And Paul Auster, fresh from Brooklyn, in his book *Winter Journal,* found his favorite Northfield spot there at its factory on Highway 19: "with its tall smokestacks pouring out white clouds of the nut-scented grain used in the recipe for that tawny, farina-textured breakfast cereal." (He might have been one of the only people who knew it was farina.) It was there, he explained, "as a slowly moving train passed by" that he and Northfield's Siri Hustvedt began to discuss whether they might spend their lives together.

Sue said that the fragrance had been outsourced to the Lakeville plant. Could this be true? Here's the thing—so much of Northfield is changing, and now Malt-O-Meal's new name is MOM—not a bad name for a place so nurturing and maternal. MOM could remain our Matriarch and Schjeldahl had been our Patriarch. Alas, its new name Multec doesn't sound like a patriarch, but more like insulated foam in a snowmobile suit. The *Carletonian Quirk,* not to be taken too seriously, announced that NEW MALT-O-MEAL SCENTED COLOGNES/PERFUMES A BIG HIT, reporting that Malt-O-Meal had unveiled a new hit product aimed at Carleton and St. Olaf College students—a hit amongst seniors who are about to leave town. The scented colognes:

> Tootie Fruities, Honey & Oat Blenders, Frosted Mini Spooners, Berry Colossal Crunch and Frosted Flakes were made for both males and females and purported to attract other Carls to wearing them. However, their attraction effects were only prevalent among college students in the town of Northfield, for unknown reasons.

In addition to fragrance, there are also the visual pleasures—the flower baskets on Division Street, those sneakers hanging on the wires in the sky that kids thought Superman had left, the runners, runners, everywhere—the thrill of seeing the St. Olaf runners all together, whizzing down the street. The Santa Run with children, adults, people running fast with Santa hats, others running to catch up. And then at the Winter Walk there were twenty-five little Santas dancing on Division Street, carefully trained for big events by Northfield's dancing school. Leslie wrote about that annual magical walk and here are a few memories from her poem by the same name:

> as though it were possible to elect
> a "Merry Christmas" for the whole icy town.
> We pause, and smile, and say what is correct.
> To our surprise, we have less urge to frown.
> A group of carolers draws near, a flock
> of turkey-red-faced, singing children. Merchants
> fling open doors, forget their gilded stock,
> come out to see how spirit switches on.
> Glad tidings are infectious. We finally don
> gaily appareled hearts, admit this time enchants,
> and smell the pines, and marvel at the stars,
> rejoicing, holding dear all that is ours.

And there were the picturesque boulevardiers without a boulevard brightening our landscape—the ubiquitous Charlie Cogan, a good Rotary man, with great ties, a big hello, and a big smile, he who used to be seen with his delightful daughter Raphaela in her Burly. And the lovely Bita (twice the winner of the secret Nordquist Princess Prize at the Party Formerly Known as Shrimp) who walked, in the summer, mistaken for Japanese when she carried a parasol, or the winter when she wore a white hat and coat to be friendly while feeding the albino squirrel in Central Park. And the pianist Marcia Widman, a welcome sight to the Northfield world as she walked from Lincoln Street to the music building at Carleton. And the two boys who ran through the neighborhood

I'm so Northfield our back stoop was the auxiliary freezer (in winter anyway). — CBS

with their yellow, blue and red Colombian flags on Colombian Independence Day. There was Jackson Bryce on that very tall bike, looking always as if he had just returned from Evensong at Oxford. And there were the male walkers, Jerry and Bill, escaping from Village on the Cannon; although sometimes dressed alike, you could tell them apart. We hadn't realized the Northfield advantage of walking until we read in the *Minneapolis Star Tribune* how seeing people walking had influenced Joe Morgan, when he was looking for a place to start a business. When Joe saw its downtown he called his wife Sherry and said: "You're not going to believe this. People are walking outside for no reason!"

There were walking groups, one of whom we might call the RealEstaters, who walked around the neighborhoods, commenting on the houses. As you know, some of our homes are mini-masterpieces upon which our humanity is written, and for others, just a place to raise the kids. This group, armed with Post-It notes, dreamed of leaving love letters or tips to the houses: "What a flawlessly restored Victorian!" "Old Buckaroo: Your ranch house is so authentic your grandmother could lasso in the backyard." "Dear Neighbor: Your house looks darling now, but Tarzan misses the jungle that used to be in your front yard." "Hey there Neighbor: What's with the fence? Raising sheep?" "Great Paint Job, Neighbor, We used to like Gray houses, now we like Green," "Love those primary colors since we miss that Norwegian primary colored look at the end of St. Olaf Avenue, and thanks for that huge chicken on your porch. Great to see it outside in the good weather and it stops us from stopping the car to peek in the window." Men from outlying farms would come walking in our neighborhoods looking for inspiration in their landscaping.

Even more exciting were the small white buses, driving Northfielders to work, or the Northfield Lines, made possible by Suzie Nakasian and the Benjamin Brothers (not a rap group). You could feel proud and patriotic to see a Northfield Lines bus parked in front of hotels in other towns. Suzie, our creative City Council member, also brought contra dancing to Northfield. In contra dancing dancers break into groups of fours, spinning around the dance floor, partners grab hands, whirl

||||||||||||||||||||||||||||||||||||||||||||||||||||||||||||||||||||||||||||||||||||||||||||||||||||||||||||||||||||||||||||||||||||||||||||||||||||||||||||||||||||||

POLICE LOG, January 23. Duck reported stranded on ice in the Cannon River.

around, and break off to find someone new. People who arrive alone are folded into a larger group, while groups that started together break apart to meet new dancers. (So Northfield.)

And the Northfield sounds—the happy sounds from the swimming pool on Fifth Street in the summer, the high school football game, fun to hear in the fall while having dinner on the porch (the deck to you), the Sunday bells that could make all of us sitting in our robes feel joyful or guilty for not heading to church, the musical bells at seven PM that Saint Dominic used to send across the river. And the trains in the night.

There were the bad sounds, the sirens, the fear in a small town that someone you know could be in trouble.

And for all you new folks, if you hear the sirens at noon on Wednesday, don't think your house is on fire—it's just a test of the city alarm system.

Try to get a house where you can hear the football game, or at least the bells. What are you building over or under? that Tyvek pink or white? Will you grow the ceiling on your living room and call it a Great Room? Will you have what we used to call a den and make it into man cave? (If you think about it, the old fashioned den also had to do with male animals.) Will you call other guys and have guy play dates on sports nights in your man cave or make up fun ways to nerd out? The good news is you can buy a man cave sign at the Mall of America for $69.95 (Barbara's Norwegian forebears in Minnesota also lived in caves when they first came from Norway. They were hearty but not primitive. You can still find their cave, but you have to wiggle through a giant cornfield.) And what about furniture? Watch out that you don't fall for that perfect harmony that Suzanne called the "Dayton's Look," named for the store formerly known as Dayton's. You'll probably need a Family Room, to hide your TV and your (messy?) real life.

THERE ARE THOSE WHO LOVE US

And sometimes, of course, when you get used to us, we'll need you Tyvek Towners to tell us what you think. Ukrainians seemed to love us:

|||||||||||||||||||||||||||||||||||||||||||||||||||||||||||||||||||||||||||||||||||||||||||||||||||||||||||||||||||||||||||||||||||||||||||||||||||||||||||||||||||||||

I'm so Northfield I set my clock to the sound of the trains. — Chris

UKRAINIAN VISITOR WILL GREATLY MISS NORTHFIELD

To the Editor:

We, Ukrainian educators, enjoyed reading the article about our experience in such a wonderful place as Northfield. Before we leave, we would like to express our gratitude, etc.

I fell in love with you at first sight. You impressed me greatly with your marvelous inner world. Your soul is unique and kindness is endless. I am always thinking of you. You have taken my heart away.

I have known you for four weeks already, but I could not reveal my feelings until this very moment. Maybe I will not see you again. I feel frustrated. I just want you to know wherever I will be, your image will follow me. You are the only one. I will miss you the rest of my life. I love you, Northfield.

Olena Fimyar, Ukrainian teacher visiting Northfield

A Tour of Downtown Northfield

LISTEN UP! IF YOU, TOO, WANT TO FALL IN LOVE WITH NORTH-field, you could use a tour. Stick with Estelle, and try her first tour, Dancing Down Division, known by our revered introverts as Dodging Down Division. They were hypervigilant folks known to keep Avoidance Diaries ("Hid from five people today"), stayed alone in their room and never came to the cabaret. They have their own book now, *Quiet*, by Susan Cain, a bestseller for years and now there's a children's edition. They would never walk downtown on Saturdays when the Peace Vigil was on Bridge Square. This vigil was quiet, although cars supported the Saturday vigil by honking, and introverts didn't mind doing that. However, when the *Northfield News* Online Poll asked whether people should be allowed to protest, demonstrate, or promote their cause in the Square, 9% said yes, but only if their activities are silent. It would be dreamy to organize Northfield's first whispering flashmob. (There's even a Massmob around the country where groups of Catholics gather to visit older but still beautiful Catholic churches.)

The Peace Vigil was important; our vigilant parents were serious, and one was known to sign her daughter's school excuse form saying: "Missy is sick of war." And so were we, even when it was far away. Alas, we have been at war ever since, unless sly Wolf Blitzer is telling everyone fibs on CNN. Does anyone still remember when Rodney King said "Can't we all get along?"

While Village Squares have become centers of political unrest and change, Bridge Square was just Northfield's comfortable living room. If you've ever lived in a town without a center, you'll remember how sad and lonely that was, and you'll kiss the ground on Bridge Square. Rob Hardy, our top choice for Northfield's Poet Laureate, immortalized Bridge Square forever in the sidewalk poem in its cement:

> On this spot
> Someone once thought of something
> Someone remembered
> Someone stopped to talk
> To someone she had not seen all winter
> Something new happened here:
> Rain fell:
> Wind tagged at someone's umbrella
> Someone persevered.

Those lines about someone stopped to talk to someone she had not seen all winter were especially appropriate, because even Rob's poem might not be seen, hidden by snow for some of the winter. Speaking of snow, if your mailperson refuses to deliver your mail on Monday because you haven't shoveled your walk after three snowy days, writing on Tues-

---

CARLETON SECURITY BLOTTER, January 24. At 1:00 am a student called to report the smoke detector in his room was beeping. Security responded with a new battery.

At 1:30 am the aforementioned student called back saying the smoke detector was still beeping. Security responded with a new smoke detector head and another new battery.

At 2:00 am the same sleepless student called back to say that the beeping was possibly coming from a different smoke detector in the same room. Paranormal activity was not suspected to be the source of the beeping. Security responded and restored both smoke detectors to normal operation.

day that: *The Persian messengers travel with a velocity which nothing human can equal... Neither snow, nor rain, nor heat, nor darkness are permitted to obstruct their speed* won't work. Nor will another message on Wednesday: *Neither snow, nor rain, nor heat, nor gloom of night stay these couriers from the swift completion of their appointed rounds.*

NORTHFIELD PUBLIC LIBRARY

Back to Estelle. She always started her tour on Division Street by the Carnegie Library. In the summer of 2012, the Library apologized for cutting down a tree. They apologized again when they asked an older person if he wanted to "check out." And you should know that now in some libraries, you can actually check out people. (That means you can check out fifteen minutes of an accountant, for example.) If you order a book now, our wonderful library puts your requests on an outside shelf—making it good for spying what everyone is reading; perhaps it could be its own little LiteraryMatch.com. We loved that little room in the children's section with all the stuffed animals, where our favorite game was protecting Minnie Mouse from the other animals, who all seemed to be male. (Later we learned that a human Minnie had been a witness when a real live Spider-Man scuffled with the police on Times Square). Our library was also special because our library director always got to be head of the swimming pool and the ice arena. Northfielders loved all their libraries and archives, and when it wasn't confidential, we especially loved hearing tales of reincarnated visitors checking out the archives to read about their previous selves. But a good word about our library. If you join the Friends of the Library, you will get the world's cutest, most lovable membership card ever, in addition to some nice discounts.

One fall day two gorillas were discovered sitting on the library wall. After the discovery that they weren't real, when asked why they wanted to be gorillas, they simply said "We're bored." But all the way up the library hill, these two bored gorillas had left a banana on every parked car, and even on a bike. Now there is a sculpture at the bottom of that

---

I'm so Northfield, my children know that you NEVER *put your tongue on a drinking fountain in winter. — Lora Forbes Applegarth*

hill on Division Street—a sculpture by high school artists, with a new mentor each year. It began with Mac Gimse, St. Olaf professor of art and art history, followed by Raphael Estrella, an artist and ceramicist, and Rick Swearer, a glass artist. Raphael, thanks for staying in Northfield after college; Rick, thanks for coming back to Northfield; Mac, thanks for being you; and Christie Clark, thanks for making it happen for its early years, and thank you, Dixon Bond, wherever you may be, for your great ideas.

ARTISTIC NORTHFIELD

The Sketchy Artist, the most original store in Northfield, was across the street from the library, full of wonders for young visitors, with colorful papers, pens, cards, and delightful objects from Japan. After the Japanese tsunami, the Sketchy Artist persuaded Northfield stores to devote 10% of a day's sales to help the Red Cross help Japan. Even the small wooden plaque on the door of the store was written in Japanese and English, and the sweetest part about it was that the Sketchy Artist had not yet been to Japan. The shop is conveniently located near the Center for the Arts, usually known as NAG, the Northfield Arts Guild. The Guild was founded in 1959, by Myrna Johnson, art professors Dean Warnholtz, John Maakestad, Dorothy Divers, sculptor and professor Ray Jacobsen, and dancer Evie Woodruff. Our first vision and memory of the Northfield Arts Guild were three women in a convertible in the Jesse James parade dressed in 1890s red taffeta showgirl dresses: Myrna Johnson, Judy Brandt, Millie Johnson, Gloria Shigley, Phyllis Faxvog, and Carol Fossum, sharing that privilege through the years. The Guild celebrated Northfield's artists month by month, and taught others beginning in childhood to be artists, musicians, writers, dancers and actors. There were shows for Arts Guild members, local artists, St. Olaf and Carleton fifth-year apprentices, and Northfield High School Honors artists, which always included an artist's statement, as well as a book for each artist so that everyone could comment and connect. They were organized and curated by Katherine Noorhis, the Northfield High School art teacher. The artists' statements from 2014 made you believe in Northfield, art, and the future in their hands.

Emma Geary, whose painted works and wood pieces provided such messages as "Pay it Forward" and "Live to be 100" wrote:

> Sometimes I look up from whatever I've been working on and I am amazed at how the world has gone on doing its thing, whether I've been participating or not... I pushed the prints and colors and pure messiness throughout my art to remind the world that life is most beautiful when it's unplanned, messy and loud. I hope you go on to live a life that's loud... Pick an item, book a ticket, and don't ask too many questions.

Jorja Thompson drew fabulous colorful birds:

> I am like a sitting bird, waiting to take off and move on to the next chapter of my life. The serenity of each bird that I paint symbolizes how I take the time to enjoy every moment before flight. It took me seventeen years to realize I want to spend the rest of my life laughing.

Kaylen Vandergon, with watercolors and Micropen drew cities of the world: Istanbul, Venice, Cologne, Singapore, and Sydney:

> For most of my life I have wondered what it would be like to live in a big city. Someday I hope to travel to see the cities I have painted, but I have not had the chance to visit them yet... As I passed through the semester, I drew some of the cities from a closer perspective to symbolize how I will soon be living in a large city.

Isabel Bilek worked in acrylic and pen, producing such works as: Serenity, Realization, Indignation, and Acceptance:

> I've traveled through life being told many things. I've heard people say phrases that tear apart a human soul and others that were so perfectly placed that they could be compared to a warm summer breeze... My paintings weave in and out of incidents in which my emotional reactions to something were indescribable, and yet I wanted to capture them. For it is not one perspective that alters my view, rather all views, that affect our experience.

Christina Kuether's artwork reflected her interests in nature and quotations. Her work, "Wolves Don't Lose Sleep Over the Opinions of Sheep" provided strong artillery for the next time any of us get criticized.

Caitlin Kelley, who grew up on a farm, had been concerned about our environment since she was very young, and wrote: "With my art pieces I want to explore these ideas through metaphor and imagining what parts of our world could look like in 80 or 90 years." Using acrylic and pen, she painted the Statue of Liberty covered up to above her waist with water.

And there was the Northfield Arts Guild theatre, which in the winter was in a cozy theatre on West Third Street, a former church, and sometimes in Central Park in the summer. There were lots of great actors through the years. We remember Bob Quanbeck, narrating *Side by Side by Sondheim*; Gordon Forbes and David Bly in *Death of a Salesman;* Charlie Black — a dog, a variety of English and Irish men, a vampire, a detective and a murderer, a striptease artist (in drag) from Venus, George Armstrong Custer, President Roosevelt, a robot, a cat, a Frenchman, a scarecrow, a fairy, a con man, Jesse James, Adam, a middle aged Lothario, and a candlestick, and finally a beloved Northfield High School teacher, who faithfully attended as many as thirty-five graduation parties each spring. NAG's talented cast members hadn't just devoted themselves to a life in the footlights. One winter performance had a great mix of two MD's, one lawyer, two high school students, a former mayor, an obstetrician/gynecologist who was also good at spandex in charge of costumes, and Marion Hvistendahl, still acting at ninety-one. The Northfield Arts Guild had some outstanding costume designers, Deb Supps and Helen Dillon, who also had delighted the audience with clothes for the Rock 'n' Roll Revival. And young Northfielders followed. We heard that Julia Bly went to Hollywood to design clothes for TV programs. Bri Seeley and Charlotte Brackee went to Florence to study at the *Accademia Italiana, arte moda design* and now have careers as designers. Fashion and food are sometimes artistic twins, and Bri's mother Eileen founded the Cocoa Bean, and Laurie Brackee, our most inventive chef and cook, was Charlotte's mother. Fashion and food have finally become part of the art world, and now finally a vital part of art history. Frances Crouter gradu-

---

I remember Thomas Market. And the Northfield Arts Guild's summer stock!!! or was it more like "theatre season?" Oliver, the King and I... all the kids dyeing their hair black, Sound of Music, and so many other successes, like Guys and Dolls! It was more awesome because my mom was frequently the leading lady and so I always felt famous through association. — Jonathan Shepard

ated to a great career in the cooking world after going to the Culinary Institute of America, went to Antarctica to be a pastry chef, then returned to be an editor of Allrecipes.com, and that website is not kidding.

OLD DIVISION STREET

You could get tired of Estelle's telling you about places that were no longer there—like the Dahl House—the place where you'd try on clothes and hide from Mrs. Dahl before she told you how great you looked when your size 14 body was squeezed into a 10. We now have Anna's Closet, named after Lucy's daughter, that has lots of 14's. Or the Ideal Café, called the Ordeal by Northfield students. Fred, the owner, warned his young staff that at the Ideal Café the customer was not king. One day when some ladies complained about the tuna sandwiches, Fred, quite surprised, testified that it had made the cat whose picture was on the can smile. But even Fred got frustrated when visited by two husky men who would come in often, sit at booth number 5, talk awhile, but never order. Many weeks later, Fred came out, and it was reported that right in front of them he planted an axe on that table at booth number 5, and it split it in two. (The softer Fred collected antique toys.)

NEW DIVISION STREET: DOWNTOWNERS

Now downtown has actual people. It once was that there were few permanent residents other than Maggie Lee, our former *Northfield News* editor and writer. Bart and Sue deMalignon started things off, converting Bob's Shoes into an art gallery and a fabulous apartment. They were Downtown's King and Queen, the center of all news bulletins, with Bridge Square as their front yard, an ability to report what happened at all the good parties, and when you were in your car and couldn't drop your mail in that drive-in mailbox Bart was sometimes there to offer.

Jesse James Cafe, Ideal Cafe, McDunn's Hardware; Thomas Market was across the street from the Corner Bar on division, Ericsson's supermarket was a lumber yard, Sibley school was in the new part of town; Carleton invited townies over to campus to throw rocks and break windows on Gridley Hall before they tore it down; chicken and egg farm in town next to the outdoor public swimming pool. — Christopher Bierman

Bart was the first to send a photo of the first Bridge Square Concert every spring. Across the street in what was the Lockwood Opera House (which when it did not pan out as an entertainment venue, was, for a time, wisely converted into a roller-skating rink) there was the first Northfield Condo. There was Jean Wakely (Luis Henrique's mother), whirling dervish, condo association president, star Mary Kay rep, Mary Jo Oberling with a wicked sense of humor, Downtown Dagmar, and Bob Tisdale, and Bob and Martha Davies, who was the daughter of the famed Florence Weichmann. Both Martha and Bob had strong interests in the Northfield Historical Society right across the street. Bob liked sitting in his reading chair on the catwalk on their second level and observing life on Division Street down below, spending no afternoon without issuing a report. Carole Christensen, the proprietor of Antiques of Northfield across the street called him her "very own personal stalker."

Northfield children, all gone, remembered their downtown the way it used to be. Paul Jenkins, in his song, *A Town Like No Other*, wrote:

> At night I'd close my eyes
> And see it all around me.
> Now though I'm far from home
> It's always here inside me.
> There's Perman's and Tiny's
> There's Three Oaks and Grundy's
> There's an Ordeal to fry up onions so pale
> And the people who live there
> Are friendly and helpful
> There's plenty of corn there
> And no chance to fail.

Still standing was Goodbye Blue Monday, a coffeehouse that sophisticates liked to call the Bleu. This place is the Real Northfield; it started with two old couches and remains our bulwark against gentrification.

I'm so Northfield that getting "Friday Bread" at the Quality Bakery was a weekly highlight. — *Mallory Easter Polk*

I'm so Northfield, I remember riding my bike down to the bakery and getting one of those massive glazed donuts. — *Lori Forbes Applegarth*

But who's gonna frown at the Cakewalk and Tandem Bagels on the same block—too delicious—or miss a peek at our favorite friendly giant bank president buying every kind of cupcake there is, maybe for lucky staff members.

Writers with laptops at the Bleu could sometimes be inspired to produce short stories by overhearing conversations and writing them down. When Susan Eggener came back on a sentimental journey, she re-absorbed the scene at Blue Monday, and couldn't resist texting her ex-husband about a conversation she had just overheard about Bangalore that was so Northfield. Ruth liked being surrounded by the chattering classes because it helped her concentrate. Our favorite author did all her work there, writing *Heather Has Four Mommies* and *The Tragedy of the One Car Family*. Blue Monday can even make taxpayers happy when they head to Leota Goodney's upstairs office, overcome with that delicious irresistible coffee fragrance that will last all day long.

On the next corner was the Rare Pair, rare for the quality of its shoes, window displays, and even more, for two Northfield sweethearts—Krin, called by some the prettiest girl in the NHS class of 1983, (a pastor's daughter) and Dale Finger (Gene's son, who made the most elegant drapes in town), owner of the Quarterback Club (with deliciousness maintained by the magnificent Estrems.) Krin and Dale were local entrepreneurs who had businesses that lasted and lasted. A woman from Castle Rock often rode her horse into Northfield just to see the Rare Pair displays for "their visionary zeal, somehow believing that displays on the Miracle Mile and on Fifth Avenue were obviously copied from Division Street." At Northfield Yarn, also with colorful window displays, store manager Vanessa Bodrie brainstormed ideas with the staff and then handed things over to Addie Rosenwinkel, a St. Olaf College graduate with "an impeccable eye."

Marlis Schmidt at the Local Joint, looked for the seasonal hook, based on inventory. "Since Rhoda was a window dresser in the *Mary Tyler Moore Show*, I've wanted to do it. I'm always thinking about the next window." And then there was Monkey See, Monkey Read, a won-

---

I'm so Northfield, I went to the Quarterback Club not just for the burgers, but also to visit the giant half football. — Brian Doughty

derful bookstore, that kept a healthy supply of local authors, including fifteen year old J.J.M. Braulick's book, *Alpha Beta: A Pictorial Guide to Attic Greek,* on the Greek alphabet. Braulick and her mother, in their other books, *Howling Vowels* and *Sometimes Y* gave their little town the charming name of Sundog, but they didn't fool us. It was Northfield.

Estelle could only provide its history, however, since the Monkey (who used to only Do) also stopped Reading and went away. Jessica Peterson White bought it and saved Northfield, because what would we Do without a bookstore? We miss Jerry Bilek, beloved in the business for many years, giving all of us a place to read silently, sell our books, have an audience and find someone who loved books as much as we did. Jerry was also brave enough, not only to dance ballet in the Wizard of Oz performance with his daughter Isabel, but also to bike in the Arrowhead 135, Minnesota's "you've-got-to-have-a-little-crazy-in-you-to-attempt-this" winter endurance race.

The bookstore is now on the same block as the Center for the Arts and Sketchy Artist. Jessica once created and owned Cottage Industry, a mecca and homestead for knitters. Her bookstore is named Content! Single names are now the way to go, following other famous women—Paltrow and Goop, Lively in Preserve. The new store promises a big welcome to cows and colleges, and to any woman who'll ride her horse in from Castle Rock.

And farther on there was Willie's Shoe Store, now owned by the amazing Randy, once a hangout for lovable town characters. Everyone loved the way it smelled inside, and the standing joke about Willie's is that you might have left your shoes there in 1978 but they'd still be waiting for you.

Across the street was the T. S. Eliot Trouser Tailors, (formerly known as the Pantorium.) And farther on was Quality Bakery, more than 100 years old. Mr. Klinkhammer bought it when he was nineteen, and the wife of the man from whom he bought it more than fifty years before

---

I'm so Northfield I thought the old grizzled guys (dare I say drunks?) sitting on the steps of the Corner Bar in their overalls in the middle of the afternoon—every afternoon—were kind of scary. — Nathan Quanbeck

had stuck around to help. And on the corner was Bierman's, the furniture store that had been in Northfield for more than 100 years.

Estelle never forgot to show everyone the old Northfield Post Office near Bridge Square. If you asked if the post office would accept your messy package, Bobbi, the one behind the counter, would say: "I AM the POST OFFICE." Bobbi finally left, but couldn't take the Post Office with her. She just *used* to be the Post Office. And that other great woman there, at the right hand window—everyone wanted to stand in her line to bond with her because wherever you were mailing your package she seemed to have a daughter there—Koreatown? State Street in Madison? Yep, Toronto. And there was the no-nonsense Motor Vehicles lady at City Hall, who would not let you accept your photo if you looked "mean" and would try, try, try again, to make you look worthy of your Minnesota license.

NORTHFIELD NEIGHBORHOODS: EASTSIDE, WESTSIDE

When tourists got tired of hearing about old buildings, Estelle would tour the neighborhoods. Starting on the West Side, there was 812 St. Olaf Avenue, built by F. Melius Christiansen, the founder of the St. Olaf choir. He lived here until he died on June 1, 1955. That was the very same day that the present occupants, Victor and Kiffi first met at the Tower Ranch camp in Rhinelander, Wisconsin, and forty years later they moved into what will always be remembered as the house that Christiansen built. There were charming miniature houses with Free Libraries at Madison and St. Olaf Avenue, and Greenvale and Linden. At 122 Plum there was a house with a Gratitude Tree in front of it, with notes written by grateful passersby: "I wish for a turtle," "All the Little Things in Life," "Life, Walking, Seeing, Hearing, Loving, Being," "I'm Thankful for My Left Shoe." At first we were afraid rain would hurt the messages in this special tree, but we discovered that they were written on thin sponges. And when you're here, go visit that tree. Gratitude might make you happy. It was Session Four in Northfield's Happy Hour class led by the remarkable Janet Lewis Muth with the hope of increasing happiness in both Northfield and Faribault, for fathers, mothers and children. And what a beautiful surprise: it turned out that the Gratitude Tree was right in front of her house. In turn, James Muth, sixth grader, made us happy when in the annual Design section of the *Northfield News*, he won Most Original, with "Get Ready for the Alpacalypse!" his ad for the Fossum Family Farms. His alpaca drawing was extremely cute. James helped to lead the way, and now every year on the last weekend of September alpaca farms and ranches all across America welcome visitors of all ages to meet their alpacas. The Fossum Family Farm in Northfield and the Red Gate Alpaca Farm in Dundas take part, letting people know they have Alpacas, inviting them to come and learn about them. Kraig and Teri Quamme of Red Gate Alpaca Farm also wanted to let the community know they would enjoy mentoring anyone interested in starting their own herd. "We get such enjoyment from sharing with people our enthusiasm for these wonderful animals." You'll be happy to know that children can adopt alpacas at the Red Gate Alpaca Farm in Dundas and also at the Fossum Family Farm.

At Woodley and Washington, there was a house on the corner that specialized in holidays. The talented owner made his own red, white and blue flag which seemed to be made of beads and hung it on a tree. It could stay there for Memorial Day and vibrate until Flag Day and the Fourth of July. This corner was even more famous for inflatables. It had Homer Simpson, and celebrated a great Halloween with skeletons. At first we thought those little headstones were meant to honor real people, until we got closer to see that they said Ima Goner and Izzy Dead. There was a little bit of Thanksgiving and then a great display for Christmas, except on some of the sad days when Santa was deflated and lay on the ground. One Northfielder liked the display so much that he left some other inflatables on their doorstep. However, sometimes holiday displays finally bring great sadness. A letter in the *Northfield News* made us feel sad long after the holiday: "To the editor: The excitement of the holidays quickly stopped for us on Dec. 29th when someone stole Baby Jesus out of the Nativity scene in our front yard. Two years ago we had our donkey and camel taken but this takes the cake."

On Woodley near Division, a new family had placed two matching putti sculptures on its high front porch, turning it into our first Northfield palazzo. On the East side on College Street, Tony and Loretta lived in the house where the Songbird Violette Brown once lived, a shrewd little woman who painted her curb yellow so no one would park there.

Loretta had worked at Village Drug and Tony worked at Lansing's Hardware. They took their picture window seriously and changed their exhibits at least once a month. And sometimes when you looked at their displays, Loretta and Tony would wave back. And there was that very sweet cottage on the corner of 4th and Winona, where Edith Stevens used to wake up her roomers announcing, "This is the Day the Lord has Made" until they got out of their pajamas. It was no longer a cottage after John and Elizabeth bought it and turned it into a *petite maison* playhouse, but then Elizabeth gave away her lascivious parrot and they moved to Minneapolis.

Yes, some come and some go. "Funny thing about leaving Northfield. You are never quite forgiven for doing so," John Perry wrote from Gloucester. "But I know of no other community in which I once lived where I could drive into town, pick up a phone, call twenty people, and say, 'Let's have a party.'" Who ever would believe that Will Healy would move over and leave us *and* Emmaus to continue his good work and never come back? The founders of the Canvas Church at one time wondered whether they should come to a town with so many churches, but after prayer and patience they knew they had been called into this corner of the world. One lady threw a dart at a map and later showed up in Northfield. She was also known for taking a cab to a party a half-block away. Della Lindquist, the 103 year old lady who rode in the 2014 Jesse James parade, came here because: "I just looked at Northfield once and I knew." Some of our best massage therapists left to join Massage Therapists without Borders. Some come, some go and some come back; there were always rumors that people who left *were* coming back, and some did, like Rick Swearer bringing Diane Angell, and the Lavenders or the Sullivans. Jim Fisher would try to predict what swallows might come back to Capistrano. After forty-one years, Allan Errington left Seattle with Sheryl and came back to the family farm. David Wellstone came back, bringing Leah and the Wellstone personality back with him.

CARLETON SECURITY BLOTTER, February 2, 12:30 am. Two students were discovered in a place they should not have been, doing what they should not have been doing in that place.

Now if you ever should decide to move, but cherish the memory of your house, Mar Valdecantos would make a drawing of it. Fred Somers, one of Northfield's prominent artists, arranged to paint Minnesotans' ancestral homes and spent two months in Sweden in a very rainy season. For Avis and Fred, every day in Sweden was a near miracle. Each time they reached a Swedish town, the rain stopped, and Fred painted in the sunshine. A Northfield family who had asked Fred to paint their ancestral home provided the address, but located it in another part of the country, and also expected only a "shed." Fred found it, painted it, and found that it was by no means a shed. These paintings often led to reconnecting with lost relatives. They later became a part of the 350th year celebration of the first Swedes in America at the American Swedish Institute, climaxed by a visit from Sweden's king and queen. Fred's paintings graced the celebration with an exhibition called "Homeland," and he became the American Swedish citizen of the year.

Estelle did other tours, and was known for Heels on the Ground, the famous Stiletto Hunt, original in Northfield, a strong competitor to the Jesse James Days hunt for the hidden horseshoe. Estelle, loyal to art interests, had spent part of her lifetime following gorgeous gay guys around in museums, and also invented the Male Gaze Tour. Some women sought the esthetic pleasure of innocent male-watching, a little like whale-watching—going to Cub so they could peek at that cute guy with the spiked hair in produce who knew from kumquats because he had lived in California. (That guy is so popular he doesn't even have to wear a name tag, and after he reads this he probably will continue to need protection.) And there was Tanner, the guy on the wait staff at the Ole Café with the spiked hair like Guy Fieri on the Food Network. Estelle was partial to product. She had the skill set for her tours but just couldn't monetize them nor incentivize her assistants. She'd get her talking points, plot points and price points all mixed up. Experienced as she was she could never find Walgreens at the intersection of Happy and Healthy. Her learning curve was not curvaceous. Her business designing Thank You for Your Thank You Card didn't last long, and no one seemed willing to join her selling hugs for a quarter on Bridge Square. And she could no longer give friends social advice after she sent a few sympathy letters with celebration stamps. She never lost her belief in entrepreneurship, and often sent the neighborhood boys out to sell snowballs.

NEARER TO NATURE IN NORTHFIELD

Locally Grown, the go-to Northfield website, suggested another self-guided spring tour as well, Love al Fresco, where reminiscing couples returned you to the sites they once loved and also made it—some that were gone, and others helpful for future planning. And just so you know, most of them were married, now and even then. Joe wrote that the Carleton Arb was a favorite of longtime married couples, especially in the summer when the students are gone and the likelihood of being discovered was more remote. Bob, another lover suggested: "The Arb is a good place... but the miles and miles of rural area surrounding Northfield are more reliable. I've never done anything within a block of Division." *Token Broad* wrote: "What, are you all nuts? I know way too many people around here. Although it was suggested to me that to hint at this subject might be a really good way to convince my significant other to build that nice little pergola or gazebo in the back yard that I've been angling for. Any alfresco frolics that I indulge in are gonna be far, far from here." Joe, who had first suggested the Arb, also agreed with Bob that "Miles and miles of rural area surrounding Northfield are more reliable. The County parks, esp the Rice County Wilderness Area, are primo." (There's something great about the word primo.)

Their cautious moderator warned them about Rooftop al Fresco. Not a good idea, apparently. Quoting from the *Minneapolis Star Tribune*: "Naked couple dies after 50-foot fall from roof. Police on Wednesday were investigating how a naked couple fell 50 feet from the roof of a downtown office building to their deaths. Clothing was discovered on the roof, leading authorities to suspect."

Solstice wondered: Does a gazebo count? How about a porch, screen porch, patio or any other assorted outdoor structure? Hot tub? Just wondering what you consider al fresco...this may change the answers."

"Ooh, yeah," their moderator answered: "All those count in my book, Solstice, as they all embrace fresh air.... even the garage."

However, last night a friend of mine told me that when she first moved to Northfield (thirty some years ago?) some of the "backyards" of the commercial buildings along Grastvedt Lane (behind the old "Jacobsen" block) were quite overgrown with bushes and trees, creating a, let's call it, zone of opportunity. I just had to mention it because, contrary to popular opinion, apparently some people did "Do It Downtown." There were a number of artists' studios in the upper floors of those buildings at that time. You know those Bohemians.

Now we still love to think of Grastvedt Lane, named after North-field's favorite plumber, the bushes now gone to make a parking lot, as a sacred space. But Bohemians? who knew? And who knew that there were artists' studios way back when? These studios are still filled with artists—Jill Ewald, Wendy Nordquist, Wendell Arneson, Nancy Carlson, Susan Crow, The Women Artist's Collective space (with Sue Hammes-Knopf and Mary Rose) Kirsten Johnson, Karen Oiseth, and Riki Kobl-Nelson.

Grown-up St. Olaf grads remembered that when winter came at St. Olaf, the vigilant housemothers could relax and no longer be concerned with what was happening at Norway Valley, that special place for under-graduate love. But, even beyond St. Olaf, how could love blossom in the winter? The greatest thing, maybe the only thing, about a relationship for women was to talk about it, to analyze it, to make it better, but you had to have a special man to do that. There was something terribly inviting about those two very small rooms with a table and two chairs in the back room of the Jesse James Gang's Hideaway on Division Street. And in good weather, try the gazebo by the Cannon River by the Archer House.

What's the deal with al fresco? Perhaps it's just a lusty celebration of the end of a hard winter. In the summer of 2013, Northfield seemed crowded with people "using the facilities" al fresco—that is, in strangers' backyards, off the bridge on the Cannon River and multiple trees on the boulevard. The climax was provided one Sunday morning by a lovely woman in fuschia top and turquoise shorts, who squatted under a big tree on Union Street, facing all the houses. (Although it's a little too late, there's now a solution for all of this—AirPnP. The owner of AirBnB was sorry he hadn't thought of it first.)

CARLETON SECURITY BLOTTER, February 11. At 1:20 am, a student contact-ed Security regarding alleged harassment between two residents of two adjacent college houses. Apparently an argument had developed over whether or not a stu-dent had the right to burn a religious book. The argument was extinguished and there was only minor damage to the book.

We decided to honor Northfield in this new celebratory endeavor, and Nathan re-named it The Uri Nation. This celebration was followed by the high school's production of *Urinetown* in the fall, beloved by all, minus that one man who wrote a letter to the *Northfield News*.

Our Way or the Highway

EVEN ESTELLE WOULD AGREE THAT MOST OF OUR STORES BEGAN with a dream. We'd see the signs go up, and hope for them. On some days we feared that they all were pop-up stores like they have in big cities. In certain years Division Street looked like one extended gift shop. We loved the grocery store you could walk to—Econo-Foods, with Kevin, the helpful manager, and Annette and Rosella and all the others. And remembering the former Red Owl store, where they once bagged our groceries, we always had a Petricka hunt at Cub, to see who might be left standing. We're not going to forget the Red Owl. Our favorite bookseller, true to both PBS and our wonderful town, said: "You know you are glad to be back in Northfield when you return from Chicago and hear someone humming the theme to *Masterpiece Theater* in the parking lot of the Red Owl." Incidentally, our best friend Shouri said that when she almost died, or thought she was dying after surgery, all she could hear was the *Masterpiece Theater* theme.

Alas, there were no tours to Highway 3. Kiffi called it Southfield. Who knew we'd finally go there? Who ever thought we'd go to Kwik Trip? But even if Michael Pollan said never to buy your food where you buy your gas, we couldn't resist those two Biblical brothers, Abraham and Gabriel at the cash registers, certainly a mother's pride. And then to find out that their brother Emmanuel was at the Kwik Trip in Burnsville, and little brother Isaiah was hoping to soon be a proud Kwik Tripper. (Now, if you've set a place and are waiting for Elijah to appear, he's still young and at least right now he's working as a cashier at Cub. He's not from the Kwik Trip family.) Say "Kwik Trip" to any smart Midwest shopper, and the answer is "Milk and Bananas." The staff is well-trained, and they always say: "See You Next Time," which they might have copied from Charlie Rose, who says that at the end of his TV program. Not far down Highway 3 was Quality Appliance, faithful to Northfield for many years. If you bought anything there from Sharon and Carl and their sons Casey and Ryan, you knew a company you could depend on for repairs with a quick phone call. Most of us had their phone number memorized. And there was Menards. Sandra liked seeing all those cars in the parking lot, comforted that they weren't all driving on Highway 3. And if you were looking for something at Menards, your best bet was to walk down each aisle saying "Help" in a very loud but not alarming voice, much as you might do in a minor fire. When you found someone, they really did know how to help, but it wasn't like those nice guys in the red vests at Ace who could take you right where you want to go. We didn't want to be a disappearing college town flanked by strip malls on Highway 3. We stopped Walmart once. Sometimes Walmart really tried. Once they bowed to parental pressure around Christmas when they pulled pairs of pink girls underwear off the shelves that were printed with the words: "Who Wants Credit Cards?" on the front and "When You've Got Santa" on the back. We fought to stop Target, splitting the town, coming up with ideas how Target might become a small store on Division Street. We wanted to protect Jacobsen's, our country general store beloved by tourists, where we could buy everything for sewing and lots of old-lady stuff. And then came Cub; we were pressed into loving our Cub and were given free tailgate signs to prove it. T McKinley, ask-

---

POLICE LOG, March 1. Suspicious Activity. A caller in the 700 block of Sibley Drive said that two unknown people were snowblowing the driveway. It turned out to be two teen boys who said they were trying to be good Samaritans.

ing when a small town stops being a small town, gave Cub its first review
in the *Northfield News.*

> For one thing, it's big. The dairy section is on Pacific Standard
> Time. The meat department raises its own cattle—on the
> premises. Northwest runs a shuttle from the bakery to the rest
> room. It's *big.* To find a jar of applesauce you need a topograph-
> ical map and Sacagawea. I spotted Hans Blix in the soup aisle
> looking for mouthwash. He'd been there three weeks and hadn't
> found a thing. Cub Foods isn't small-town—it *is* a small town.
> Frozen Foods just elected a mayor and a city council. Bottom
> line, when you shop Cub for dinner, you'd better pack a lunch.

(Joan Reitz, once describing our Northfield lives, said that we were
surrounded by Giants. Cub had taken Joan seriously and, according to T,
knew how to feed them.)

> Big stores sell big food: six-pound cans of creamed corn and
> gallon jugs of blue cheese dressing; barrels of ketchup and cis-
> terns of pickles; bags of Tidy Cat big enough to deodorize the
> African prideland. At the entrance to the store is a sign that
> reads, "To better serve our customers, we reserve the right to
> limit quantities." Tell that to the lady trapped in the gravita-
> tional field of a crate of Rip-L-Chips. Small towns are about
> moderation; at Cub, it's all the potato buds you and the Seventh
> Armored Cavalry can carry.

> Then there's selection. Fabric softener dryer sheets come in
> more than a dozen different scents, including "Redwood For-
> est" and "Summer Breeze." I'm sticking with my usual: "Time to
> Change My Shirt." I saw a zillion flavors of pudding, including
> something called "X-Treme Jell-O." How wiggly do you need
> that stuff to be? I imagine putting my kids in goggles and knee-
> pads for dessert. Then there's the global village: Spanish cheese,
> Thai peppers, Mexican tortillas, Chinese herbs—a shock to
> people who think of French fries and Canadian bacon as inter-
> national cuisine. In sum, unlike many small towns, Cub offers
> both variety and cultural diversity.

> For all of that, small-town humor still thrives at Cub. I over-
> heard one woman joke that the green bananas she'd put in her
> cart at the start of her visit were now almost perfectly ripe. I
> suggested she try that with a bag of grapes. "By the time you
> check out, you might have a nice zinfandel!'" She laughed po-

litely and then hid behind a two-story flat of toilet paper. I felt right at home.

The lines at the cashiers are perhaps the most stressful. First of all, the registers are located right next to an actual bank, in the event you need a loan to cover that cubic hectare of Pampers [the bank finally left in July 2014]. At the register you can also enter to win a Polaris ATV with enough horsepower to tow your cart to the parking lot. A large banner reads, "Thank You for Saving at Cub." Judging by the incessant, staccato beeps of the price scanners, I'd say there was a whole lot of spending going on, too.

The checkers are trained to ask, "Did you find everything you wanted today?" At this, the guy in front of me — a tough-looking hombre with a leather Harley jacket and serpentine tattoos — broke down completely. "No! Nothing!" he cried. "I just thank God I found *you!*" A nurturing sort in a red polo shirt emerged from customer service and led him, still sobbing, to the pharmacy. We're pretty sure he'll be all right.

Then it was my turn. Did I find everything I wanted today? Having gone to school on the guy before me, I knew to lie: "Sure did!"

The checker froze, her jaw dropping in amazement. "Really?"

"Absolutely," I said. "Piece of cake." The people behind me in line gaped in awe. The checker beamed congratulations, slapping a gold star on the lapel of my jacket and handing me a coupon for X-Treme Jell-O. My fellow shoppers burst into applause. Signing autographs amid the fluttering confetti, I realized that Cub Foods isn't so overwhelming after all.

And it really isn't. Corporations might swell small towns, but they can't displace them.

I'll shop Cub, socialize with my neighbors, and help organize search parties for their children. "I spotted them near pet supplies! Send up the chopper!" We'll all master Cub, stroll its boulevards and avenues, save on massive bulk-food purchases, and occasionally experiment with Jamaican bread and Portuguese fish. The soul of Northfield isn't really changing. Like our waistlines, it's just getting a bit bigger.

T also loved the huge green dumpster in the Cub parking lot that once said: YOUTH RECYCLING BOX. "On days when my kids are really acting out all I have to do is remind them that they can be dropped off at any time."

Even some of us old-timers finally accepted Cub, but were always afraid of being knocked over by those little carts for Customers in Training. Still, who wouldn't want to go to the grocery store; baby-watching there was even better than bird-watching and it was the only place you could see real live babies in the winter. Olivia Fantini, another Northfield sidewalk poet, wrote about it:

> Laughing baby in the supermarket
> Shaking a box of animal crackers
> Too much life for one shopping cart
> Your toothless smile
> Has thrown me a life raft.

T McKinley was once new to our town, then left, and then came back to love Northfield even more: "I love stores where the cashiers ask how I'm doing—and really want to know." (REALLY?).... "I love that Northfielders—even some I don't know—wave to me as we pass in our cars.

"I love the Knights and the Dukes. I love taking my son to soccer on Monday and Wednesday evenings and seeing thousands of kids tearing around, followed by their bewildered parents lugging water bottles, snacks and collapsible chairs. The most bewildered parents find themselves coaching. Look at any team picture.... The coaches look like they're lost in the Mall of America."

BUILDING TRUST IN YOUR NORTHFIELD INFORMANTS

But really, all you new people, why should you take advice from us? We're old, almost a different species, like wallabees or manatees. We didn't even know how to get our head around anything. In fact, Ann, admired by all of Northfield for a voice that rang out at basketball games,

POLICE LOG, *March 28. 911 call. Dispatch received an accidental 911 call from a location in the 300 block of E. 6th Street. A child had accidentally sat on the phone.*

admitted that even she felt "ninety-one-ish." We are so old that most of our favorite artists and authors are dead and have now been retroactively pronounced gay. We're the formerlies. And when our children come home, as Linda said, they may find out that the old gray mère is not what she used to be. Our report here might not be thorough because we've stopped that narcissistic compulsive journaling and stick to a sentimental review of our lives from our Visa bills stapled together. We don't do enough crossword puzzles so we're now having to read *Alzheimers for Dummies* (616.831 SM). Still, we were cheered up some days about getting old, as on the day Deane Barbour watched Charlotte Dunham's eighty year old mother try out a skateboard on Winona Street. We thought it was a hallucination until Corinne Heiberg said she saw it, too.

We're dripping with Northfield Nostalgia, which in Greek was once defined as pain from an old wound. Nostalgia had been considered a mental disorder beginning in the seventeenth century. And there's the Portuguese word *Saudade* that describes an even deeper emotional state of nostalgic or profound melancholic longing for an absent something or someone that one loves, which often carries the knowledge that the object of longing may never return. However, we know that nostalgia makes people more generous to strangers and more tolerant of outsiders — *that's you!* Couples feel closer and look happier when they're sharing nostalgic memories. On cold days, or in cold rooms, people use nostalgia to literally feel warmer — *you'll need it.* And for Northfielders, nostalgia helps us remember that Northfield is a treasure and nostalgia a way of treasuring our lives.

But every town is simultaneously a seedbed of progress and a hothouse of nostalgia. You're a real Northfielder, *so* Northfield when you mourn the disappearance of a familiar spot. You'll swallow hard when you realize that a tobacco shop has replaced Jerry's antique store, that the bookstore where all the nerdy high schoolers loved to be is now a fabulous cooking store, that the popular Lansings Hardware is now a bank. You remember when you and your new boyfriends would close restau-

|||||||||||||||||||||||||||||||||||||||||||||||||||||||||||||||||||||||||||||||||||||||||||||||||||||||||||||||||||||||||||||||||||||

I'm so Northfield I remember when the only fast food we had was the Quarterback Club and a fancy dinner was All You Can Eat Chicken Wednesday at Country Kitchen. — Christopher Forbes

rants, talking into the night, the last ones to go, and now all those restaurants closed themselves forever. Tiny's and your beloved Guatemalan restaurant with Mrs. Barrientos have disappeared. Damage has been done to your town and somehow to the history of your life. The subjective landscape of your memory and desire had been built on that fragile infrastructure of economic reality. This is also true when you walk past the houses where people you loved once lived. You remember the nights that every room in their house was blazing, or when each room had its own candle at Christmas. You see the children's names and birthdates still preserved in the cement driveway, and remember when their mother and father got divorced and everyone moved away.

Put us together with you, Tyvek Towners, and it's the March of Time in reverse, like the Carleton reunion march to the chapel that starts following the Carleton alumni children, with the oldest class first, in rickshaws or convertibles or golf carts, and then all the others marching behind, sometimes in matching costumes. (Deane heard about someone who decided not to come to her reunion because everyone was supposed to dress like penguins.) And then on to the early years of parents with strollers, and then the carefree class, making the most noise. You, dear new friends, are the carefree class, that is unless you've come to be with your grandchildren. But who wouldn't want to come here and watch Astrid, Joey and Edward and Zoë and Celeste grow up?

SMALL PLANETS AROUND THE NORTHFIELD SUN

When we talk about Northfield, we're also talking about all the smaller towns that surround it, and keep it normal, even if that means making fun of it. There's Castle Rock, Dennison and Dundas, Kenyon and Kilkenny, Lonsdale, Nerstrand, Randolph, Stanton, Waterford and Webster. Some of us haven't seen these places yet, but we've learned to live with this rural sprawl. It all began with the infiltration of wildlife — squirrels, rabbits, songbirds and other cuddly creatures, and then wild young people who wanted to live off the land. Now they seem to be

I'm so Northfield I used to tell Dundas jokes. — CGF

the advance guard of invasions by deer and beavers and possums. We're
getting too close to nature. There's snow season, then ant season, then
mosquito season, followed by wasp season outdoors at the Tavern, then
bat season and mouse season, followed by bat hibernation season. As
Marion Anderson, Rice County Extension, said: Every season brings
its own stains and cleaning problems—problems that may even have
ethical or political dimensions:

Mice

This poem is about mice; its thesis is that
maybe, if you cannot beat them, you should join them.
But it's more complex than that. Sympathize!
They suffer mightily in the cause of us.
They are drafted in the fight against diseases
you can name and that are funded.
They run mazes to provide cartoons and hilarity
for us who are also running mazes without
cheese or comfort at the finish line.

Mice colonize outboard and lawn mower engines
providing warmth and safety for their offspring
and endless employment for small engine mechanics.
Mice inspire bloggers, those who would help us
deter or rescue them. What we owners of the engines
most deplore is the mouse diaspora—widespread
and long-lasting. It may signal the apocalypse.
Boat owners are not sure whether this flood
of rodents follows or precedes fire.

I empathize with the damned mice in a way.
The are only trying to survive, which I did not
understand until the last financial downturn.
"So let the mice inhabit my engine," I said.
And then I spent $236.55 on cleaning
a mouse-infected carburetor, and I joined
the brute who would exterminate them all,
like manic Kurtz in *The Heart of Darkness*.

But I suspect the Far Right doesn't read Conrad:
It might confer on them the alien mantle of thought,
which, once experienced, like mice,
is difficult to shrug off.

Robert Tisdale

Dundas, the temple of hip, is now our Brooklyn. It became famous in earlier days as a place to drink at the comfy Marguerite's, which was later transformed by Marguerite's son, Larry Anthony into the L and M Bar—L for Larry and M for Marilyn, his wife. Larry hoped to create what he called a "caring environment" and he did it—a bar for more than 130 years deserves love and respect, and we should care for it in turn. There's a game room, there's Marguerite's patio, Northfield's favorite al fresco dining spot (yes, dining and drinking only.) Larry once thought it was the "best kept secret" in Rice County, but now all the best people know about it. There's a great print of the L and M by Alexander Hage. You can find it in the Weisman collection at the U of M, or Google it under Twenty Views of Dundas. Dundas, like Brooklyn, became a destination for gourmet restaurants. Larry sold the bar to some other great people, and Larry said he had enjoyed having Northfield as a suburb.

We're happy to be a small town, surrounded by other small towns, surrounded by farms. For some of us, we haven't explored and are continually amazed by all the beautiful green land on each side of the highways, acres and acres, but the farms sustain us, keep us humble, let us see ourselves perhaps as creatures of comedy. An agritour, or even a CSA tour similar to the old Marston Headley Northfield tours might be an eye-opener. Farms bring us joy on holidays—pumpkin patches, hayrides and sleigh rides. We now have the Red Barn, serving pizzas from May through October, and even Barn destination weddings. Pat Winter, who with his wife owns this great place, found that "when brides walk into the barn, they immediately look up to the rafters, surprised; they have often not been in a barn, but they knew they wanted to have their wedding in one. It's mysterious to them. It's part of their past they don't

CARLETON SECURITY BLOTTER, April 7. At 6:30 pm, an impish water balloon assault at Musser Hall left one laptop computer in need of a towel.

know anything about." Sandra, although she planned to spend her last days there, said that Valley Grove marriages sometimes don't last. Barn weddings, however, seem primal and enduring. (Report back.)

Elizabeth O'Sullivan, a truly remarkable writer, brings the life of the farm to us, stories of children and pigs and chicks:

> The chicks that we picked up at the post office in December have grown from adorable little fluff balls into regular hens. They're much smaller than our grown layers and aren't producing eggs yet, but they have all their feathers and one of them is trying to crow.
>
> This week, a few have been venturing outside for the first time. It clearly takes some courage for them to step out into a new world, and most aren't interested. A few are willing to take the risk though, especially some Delawares, which are cream-colored with pretty black accent feathers.
>
> [And later:] I cried when I took them to be turned into stewing hens. We'd raised them since they were fuzzy chicks, and I recognized all the individual, quirky birds. I talked with them every day for almost two years, enjoying their comforting, crooning comments.
>
> My one comfort was that a few of my favorite birds left to start a second career as models. They joined the little flock of chickens kept by Glynnis Lessing, a ceramic artist who lives just north of town. All her chickens are black and white because she makes black and white pottery, and some of it is graced with pictures of chickens.
>
> I can understand why an artist would want chickens. The birds have a hilarious way of being graceful and awkward at the same time. People share this trait with chickens, but it is harder for us to laugh at ourselves because our awkward moments are so painful.
>
> Chickens, on the other hand, never seem embarrassed. After being forcefully reminded of its place in the pecking order, a chicken just ruffles its feathers to clear its thoughts, then moves on with chickenly dignity.
>
> Watching them do this is almost like witnessing redemption.

All their grace and awkwardness are on full display, too. Sometimes a demure little hen will remind me almost of a swan with her lovely-curved neck and the delicate way she carries herself.

The chickens I have seen on Glynnis's pottery make me smile, too, because they remind me of that same wonderful joke. I feel she sees that same beautiful blend of grace, awkwardness and chickenly dignity. Then she puts it on display so people can appreciate it.

My chickens that now work as models might nourish people, just as surely as the chickens that will be eaten in warm, nourishing stews. As much as our bodies need good food, our hearts sometimes need to be reminded that we—along with our chickens—are graceful and awkward at the same time and that even this can be a source of joy.

I learned as a child that anyone who falls in love with a chicken is bound for heartbreak.

(Elizabeth constantly reminds us: Hey, Northfield, lots to learn.)

NORTHFIELD FASHION

We liked thinking of ourselves as living near farmland and living simply (there's a magazine for that) with no showing off. You can see it in the clothes we wear. Northfielders often seemed to wear matching costumes. The "Northfield Dress" was sort of like those Mormon dresses but with short sleeves and no waistline—Yearning for Zion dresses without the polygamy. Sandra called them pottery dresses, not made of clay, but in earth tones, worn by women who probably collected ceramics. But here's a tip. If you're invited out, even to a supersize soiree in Northfield, dress down and then dress down again.

Years ago, many of these women had their "colors" done, absorbing the wisdom of "Colour Me Beautiful" and never strayed. They were either fall, winter, spring or summer, and you could see them from afar in their rich brown, apricot, deep green or heavenly blue. But even they must know that you can't even judge an egg by its color.

When they had to make a decision about purses or bags, they read *Vogue* in the library and decided those new gorgeous, thousand dollar designer bags must be from Fairyland, and they'd need a purse-wallah or even a husband to carry them. (Their friend Jim was known for carrying a friend's purse on his cruise to Greece because it was so valuable that someone might steal it, but relax, that woman was from Arizona.) Northfielders settled on the Northfield high-status tote, the purple one from Just Food. Those Just Food fans kept trying to tell people that becoming a locavore didn't just mean that you stopped shopping at Byerly's. If you haven't joined Just Foods, join up. They've got ceremonies and will ring a cowbell and announce your name.

But for young and old, the real generation gap was the 8½ inches between where the chest stopped and a few inches below the navel—the new bare part—the omphala style. It's not so prevalent now, but in the beginning when young women didn't own those kind of pants or skirts, they'd just roll the waists down a bit. It caused a boom in undershirts. This fashion also produced derriere decolletage, an accidental guilty pleasure, sometimes finished off with a tattoo. Crosses were good. (Jan, trying to remember what made her happy, remembered that she was grateful that she didn't have a tattoo.) President Obama thought about them, too: "What we've said to the girls is, 'If you guys ever decided you're going to get a tattoo, then mommy and me will get the exact same tattoo in the same place. And we'll go on YouTube and show it off as a family tattoo.'" And sometimes these tattooed flying buttresses when covered were marked with the mysterious words, Aeropostale.

Fashion didn't end with the young. The fashionistas at Millstream Commons still maintained their high standards. Kathleen Flynn would not only personally layer herself with jewelry but would glitz up her walker with lights and a holiday-themed décor. Kathleen styled herself after Jackie O and the pictures of her as a young woman and as a career woman are stunning. And there was the remarkable Fritzi who had been a fashion buyer in New York, and an artist who after having

---

CARLETON SECURITY BLOTTER, April 25. At 10:55 pm, A college employee reported an accident between a college-owned lawn mower and a college employee-owned car after the mower threw a rock through the vehicle's rear window.

accidentally dropped the adjective "hideous," hoped to use her talents to help the Millstream staff dress. She suggested pencil skirts, fitted jackets and heels. When the staff protested that they needed to be comfortable, Fritzie quoted her own mother who had said: "You can be comfortable when you're dead."

Millstream ladies also had their own secret Smoky Point II, far from the building.

Now, Tyvek Towners, we guess you know you're strangers here yourself. Smoky Point was across from the Middle School, which was once the High School. It was reserved for secret smokers, with the name "engraved" on the sidewalk. When Shouri and Krittika bought their house at 320 Union, we didn't carry out our dream to give them some stationery that had the distinguished name of Smoky Point written in large letters on the top.

Some Northfield residents would proudly wear head-to-toe Clothes Closet, that adventurous place once run by the tattooed Jane Greenwood, wild about horses, who spent fourteen years of her adult life as a comedian with Dudley Riggs, and later joined up with many charitable organizations. And there was Used A Bit, run by the Senior Center, where some older citizens could buy stuff that other downsizing older ones were smart enough to discard. We loved to count the bread machines in the kitchen section. Pre-owned was the new new. That handsome Mr. Touchette volunteered there, and the fashionable Jean Larson and the lovable Linda Stadler, a woman so fabulous that even her supervisor cried in public when she retired. Some younger customers would inquire whether that young man who worked there from time to time was unattached. Used A Bit was distinguished by Kristi, an interior decorator who managed the place, and made everything look irresistible.

So Northfield-centric, we were all dressed up with nowhere to go. But everywhere we went, we might be followed in restaurants by an attractive group of happyish women all in red hats, who could fill a big table. Few other women wore hats, but there were two at the UCC. Leota Goodney found that she liked surprising people who never expected a Certified Public Accountant to go places in a fancy hat. Rather moody,

I'm so Northfield I lived a block from Smoky Point. — CBS

Leota needed seventeen hats to match her mood—among them, a black feathered one for funerals, and a white Queen Mum hat. And then Jan Stevens, in real estate and in Rotary, knew that a hat could give one more authority, but "if it isn't magical you can't wear it."

We were old enough to be around when pantyhose, the greatest invention of that century, were discovered. When Beth, a Carleton student, interned at a pub, patrons there always wanted to know: "Tights or Stockings?" Modest Northfield women even wore pantyhose under their slacks to prevent jiggling. Where, where might the tender whiff of sensuality be hiding? Maybe it was in shoes—those peek-a-boo shoes, the peep-toe décolletage of the v-shape, showing just a bit of toes, making us want to see more.

And where were the polka dots and buttons and bows, empire styles, on maternity clothes? Now those happily expectant women wore fitted belly T-shirts, loudly announcing: "Hey, Look at Me. I didn't forget to have a baby."

And remember, Tyvek Towners, Northfielders meet through fashion signals. Marion Rankin McKenzie met Nancy Moyer (Mike's Bike mom) when she saw a new woman in a long Stewart kilt walking outside Marion's store on Division Street. She tapped on the window. The kilt did it, and they became close friends, sharing their Scottish heritage. Marion later married Karl Rolvaag, son of Ole Rolvaag, who in his novel, *Giants in the Earth*, captured the hopeful spirit of Northfield, when a pioneering farmer gives a visitor a tour of his land, describing his beautiful home and his large buildings. The visitor confesses that he can't see them. "That's because they haven't been built yet," the farmer acknowledges, but they already exist as reality in his mind. If you want to see a real Ole Rolvaag home, take Estelle's tour and stop at 311 Manitou.

ART IS EVERYWHERE

In the near future, Northfield could become an arts colony. Not too many years ago there were plans to renovate the old Middle School into a colony of artist studios. This did not happen, although it did become a Center for Creativity. It still seems a dream to think of them all there. There would be Jan Shoger, who has given so much of her life to artists, not only as a teacher, but also organizing and promoting other artists at the Northfield Arts Guild. Jan's art has taken many interesting turns, work after being in Japan, a retirement show devoted to her work at St. Olaf, prints, and now very exciting watercolors of nature, which became wilder and wilder. Tim Lloyd, who worked in silver, has one of his Japanese-inspired silver teapots in Washington, DC's Renwick Gallery. Dave Mahachek brought new excitement to the Northfield art world when he established Art.Org in a new gallery. And later we had a new charter school, ArtTech, which attracted not only students in the arts, but exciting, non-conventional students. Its name is now Arcadia, which has often served as a name for an idyllic utopia. Artists kept coming through the years. David Peterson, who worked both in wood and metal, came in the last few years. Toni Easterson brought textile arts to Northfield, and Kirsten Johnson brought wild exciting colors in her work.

Sharol Nau became a versatile artist, interesting here as an example of the artist's never standing still; her first plunge at art work was for a Square Inch show in Rochester; art at Northfield's Chicken Coop Gallery followed. A turning point in her career happened in New Mexico, painting in a place where the light was strikingly different, with reflections off the desert. Her later work was devoted to shelter belts, trees that were planted to protect farmland from the wind. She took a new creative direction when she suggested, as part of a grant, a River Curtain strung across the Cannon River. The idea was born with scribbling on a piece of paper, with a concept of stringing the curtains over the river so they would float in the air, float like sheets on a clothesline. Photos she had taken of Heath Creek played out in this work as well. In the last years she found yet another inspiration in mathematics, after she attended her first Math in Art Conference at Stanford. Loren Larson, a professor of mathematics, in turn, had retired into art, designing vari-colored wooden trays and other objects, that also illustrated mathematical principles. If you stopped to admire them for a few minutes you could get a free math lesson, even on the street. Sharol's interest in mathematics then led her to inspirations from Mayan art work based on numbers, and on re-

CARLETON SECURITY BLOTTER, April 28. At 8:15 pm, Security responded to Myers Hall to check on a student that had injured themselves while practicing gymnastics on a towel bar.

markable and exciting work with books: folded books, curled pages, parabolas, and freely formed books not using mathematical problems. These works somehow appealed to everyone who loved books, and were sculptural as well. Prints, drawing, painting, mathematically-inspired abstract art, photography, river curtains. What remained? Well, Sharol had not tried sculpture until she produced Cementitious Fall(s) at Art.Org in Northfield, Minnesota.

Paul Krause, Northfield's art videographer, produced some memorable programs honoring the work of Northfield's artists. A production about Ray Jacobsen's sculpture brought enthusiastic crowds to the Northfield High School auditorium and the very moving story of Fred Somers' work at St. Paul's Carondelet Village was a favorite at the Weitz. These stories later appeared on Minnesota Public Television.

POETS: ON SIDEWALKS, ON PAPER, AT READINGS

Poets and writers were everywhere in Northfield—on the sidewalk, reading at Monkey See, Monkey Read, taking Northfield with them to other places. Brendon Etter had been known to write a play every day, and David Bly (perhaps before helping Minnesota in the legislature) wrote a poem every day. If you think about it, why should you be concerned about publication when your poetry could be on the sidewalk, perhaps lasting forever. However, mind your step, it feels sad if you walk on top of a poem on the sidewalk, just as you used to break your mother's back by stepping on a crack. It could be exciting to keep wet cement ready for visiting poets from Big Cities to write one of their masterpieces on our sidewalk, just like Grauman's Chinese Theater.

There was the poem on the library hill (a perfect setting)

> Do not be afraid
> Of letting your mind
> Wander

written by Lilly Hanlon, a ten year old, who understood twenty-first century neuroscience. The beauty of the Sidewalk Poetry selection was that it was open to writers of all ages and abilities. It stimulated appreciation and new work. Winners have ranged from age 10 to 70+, with grade schoolers, middle-schoolers, high-schoolers, college students and teachers, many adults, experienced and first-time poets alike. A staff member from the Chaska Women's Correctional Facility took photos of each poem with her little camera and created a project for the inmate women with them. She had them blown up to pavement size, distributed them around the walled exercise area to create a Poem Walk for all the women. They were able to talk about their favorites, and had chances to write their own poems. Leslie Schultz, who was on the Arts and Culture Commission with Philip Spensley and Bonnie Jean Flom, spoke of her gratitude, realizing the power of poetry, the human need for it, and the truth that you never really know how the good things you intend and try to do might echo or ripple far beyond your own time and place. And consider what it did for the new writers as well. Martha Paas, who spent her career as a teacher and scholar, (with a poem that can be discovered on the south side of Second street between Division and Highway 3) found that the project helped her return to a love of poetry she'd set aside as she entered graduate studies, a love she can now share with her granddaughter.

When Leslie read her poem at the Poem Parade by the Dufours Cleaners, it was getting late. As she read: "Tonight a red star/catches in the elms/The moon burns/on the horizon/The whole world glitters,/ even my breath" it was a magical moment when she was able to gesture to the nearly full moon rising over Econofoods (as it often did) to the east.

Matthew Fitzgerald, a Carleton student, read his poem that begins: "My father asked me if I wanted the farm." His parents were there, and he said that the poem had arisen because his father had asked him this. When someone in the audience asked about his answer, he said that he had not yet given it. Here somehow was a whole true novel, a Midwestern multigenerational epic, condensed into a sidewalk poem.

There were some poems that you'd never forget, that seemed to ring in your head forever, especially when you're lucky enough to hear them

---

CARLETON SECURITY BLOTTER, May 11, 1:30 am. A larger-than-lifesize Fiberglass horse was observed in front of Cowling Hall. It apparently had galloped off by the time Security was able to return to the scene.

at a poetry reading. There was an unforgettable stanza in Susan Jaret McKinstry's poem, "Legacy":

> Now a daughter, an orphan, a mother
> my legacy is the raincoat. Shapeless
> when I pull it from my suitcase,
> it fills her form when I put it on—perfect fit,
> our size the same until she shrank into illness
> I feel like her.
> It was her suburban uniform
> In all seasons of Chicago rain. I find
> Her business card, a crumpled dollar and a shopping list
> In one pocket, Kleenex in another.

(Somehow it was that special touch, the Kleenex that kept it fresh in memory.)

Or "I am a tough cookie," in Sigi Leonhard's poem "Tough Cookie," although sometimes it was hard to remember which Tough Cookie had written it.

And there was Penchant, our most beloved poetry group, women who had been together writing poetry since the 1970s. Karen Wee, one of the group's founders, in later years made her early South Dakota ranch life come alive—what a thrill for many of us just stuck forever in our Victorian houses thinking about women's issues—

Circles

> Dad showed bulls in Denver in 1946
> I was six and taught to lead them
> in the show ring by a halter
> and short rope—one by one—before purchase
> by men in Stetsons smoking cigars
> who thought perfect—

> Who knows what they thought—
> all that muscle mass and testosterone led around
> a cattle show ring by a small girl
> in leather chaps and cowgirl boots
> I remember the smell
> of urine and manure mixed with straw—

The look in my father's green eyes—
my lack of fear—and haunting
pungence in the ring-round-rosy-we-fall-down
of life

For Northfield, these poems were exotic, as exotic as a life in South
Dakota could be. We wanted a book. There was "The Bull Ride," "Blue
Boy—Registered Black Angus Bull," "The Old Barn," and one about
Oscar the hired man.

Jane Taylor McDonnell joined the women poets after a career as a
writer and professor, describing poetry as her first love. She wrote about
many places she had been in the world, but so many of her poems were
tributes to deep relationships—with her parents, Southern aunts, children, grandchild, and friends.

It's been said that some of Marie Gery's poems "inhabit" Jane Gibson, better known as Jane Euphemia Gibson. After previously portray-
ing James' mother, Zerelda, for so many years, Marie wanted to become
someone else who was like her—educated, single, opinionated, street
smart, but with a sense of humor and not so angry. And then Marie remembered Zenobia, the librarian in the small town where she grew up.
Later in 1955 at the University of Iowa Marie's summer room mate, Jane
Gibson, opened a whole new world to her. Both were waitresses in the
dining room at Currier Hall that summer, a time when Iowa teachers
returned to school for one reason or another, and Currier was the only
women's dorm available. After nine months of being in charge of a class-
room, these teachers wanted only the best service, *the* best service without the addition of a tip. Putting Zenobia and Jane together offered an
exercise in delight and she began to turn some of Jane's observations in
to poems:

...Not much goes on here I don't know about.
People talk in small towns....
Politics and school keep most of us busy
and church, of course, and circle, and the book club.
Some lady up at the university is fussing
about the effect romance novels have on women.
Seems to me Justine and Margaret breathe
a trifle faster after chapter four,

but that's probably good for their systems.
Frankly at our age, breathing is about as good for you
as almost anything...

Out here on the prairie, newcomers think
their stay will change things.
About the only thing ever changed around here
is diapers....

And later:

I believe we feel about art in the schools
like we feel about art in our lives.
Both are fine as long at they don't cost anything.
... we hold with art and God
we just don't trust either one of them.
What would happen if people believed
they could accomplish something wonderful
without being plugged in or declared a winner?
What if everybody went out alone of an afternoon
down to the lake and watched the waves
lapping up the sand on the shore,
saw a mother duck count her hatch and some fish jumping?
Why, not a soul would take any notice, and I do believe
we like to think of ourselves
as a noticeably progressive community.

These poems seem to speak to us, maybe because they're plain-spo-ken, remind us of our own town, and because it seems that Jane could easily be someone we know or want to know.

Mary Lewis Grow, in yet another poetry group, found us on a special day when she had just finished writing:

"When I am Old" was always a distant future,
a place inhabited by others.
But now it is my home,
a landscape littered with fallen trees and limitations.
And yet... new green shoots push through the rotted leaves
And bare boughs are decked with wild new beginnings:
Bright teal eyeglasses and the anchor for a zip-line.

It's clear that our poets cherished their welcome in Northfield. Rob Hardy III, following a serious cross-country ski accident, said that the only good thing that had come from it was when the ER doctor said: "Oh, you're Rob Hardy, the poet." It finally came about that some of our poets just couldn't stop themselves from just being poets. They wanted to be painters, photographers, skateboarders, actresses, dancers, scholars, or priests.

Riki Kölbl Nelson, co-founder of the Northfield Women Poets not only wrote poems but was also an exciting artist, with her work sometimes reminding us of one of her first poems, her juvenilia, which started with the idea, so characteristic of that era:

> I am a mean woman
> I am mean, mean, mean
> the only ever time
> that I ain't mean
> Is when you lick
> my anger clean
> and love me
> to the bone.

created an essential Riki, the Rooster Woman, and the Northfield Women Poets' collections, *Absorb the Colors,* and *Tremors, Vibrations, Enough to Rearrange the World,* continued to feel Riki-esque, describing her vibrant paintings as well. *Penchant,* published in 2007, came from Karen Wee's poem PenChant.

We went away one year and came back to find the Northfield Women Poets changing Northfield around the same time of Women's Liberation, both changing the town in many ways. Changes could happen when you leave, but no Northfielder was allowed to change too much without going away for a year or so. One woman came back, had lost some weight, and would be remembered in that special year as someone who could shoehorn herself into size 2 jeans. Mary Easter was perhaps

CARLETON SECURITY BLOTTER, May 11, 4:50 am. Having found its way to Nutting House, the horse was again observed by Security. Again, it managed to disappear before being captured.

the only Northfielder who continued to reinvent herself. She seemed to dance for us forever and in *Dancer at Fifty-Three*, she writes of that life:

> But sometimes, for seconds, now,
> the ghost of that racing dancer
> enters this body and I fly again
> breathing twenty-year-old breath
> singing through loose joints
> in love with the world

Mary was a choreographer, taught dancers, wrote a book as well as short dramas about her ancestry, joined Penchant when it was the Northfield Women Poets and wrote some remarkable poems, and in the middle of all that, modeled, designed and made sweaters, and carried her glorious voice to the church choir.

There was Leslie Schultz, a photographer and a poet.

April was Poetry Month and scattered around Northfield were poetry boxes, so that you could choose a poem you liked, and put poetry in your pocket. St. Olaf had a poetry house, hosted one year by men and another by women, providing a great location for creative minds to meet on campus, and mentoring young poets at the Northfield Key.

Poetry could be found everywhere. T McKinley, in "Life According to Community Ed" (that wonderful publication that brought us Puppy Head Start) gave us a found poem, made up of the first lines from course descriptions:

> We all spend most of our days getting things done.
> And using the rational part of our minds
> Do you like Asian food?
> Do you suffer from over-packers
> Syndrome?
> Why study Italian?
> Ever dream of creating stunning
> Scrapbook layouts?
> Using black and white pages side by
> Side?
> School, work or play—
> Come and join the fun as you race down
> the hill on a snow tube

Looking to get into shape, have fun and
Meet new people?
    Learn this ancient, but still popular game
    In a relaxed, non-competitive
Environment.
    It's time to play
    Bring a partner to learn to do massage at
Home
    Spend an evening with your partner and
Explore ways to grow
    Do you need a tutor?
    Snuggles is ready for c-c-cold weather,
Bundled up in his hat, mittens and scarf
    It may be winter here, but it is summer
Down under!
Babies really change our lives, don't they?
    We know when babies and toddlers want
something... but what is it?
    A traditional mound centerpiece with candles
    Can you imagine how many kinds of farm equipment you
and your child can explore?
    First aid can save a life!
    Grandparents, learn more about the
parenting your children are providing
    Learn the tricks!
Bring your children for food
And family fun.

And at Carleton's Willis Hall, where custodian Randy Peck worked at night, he wrote about Lucy. Lucy was a skeleton, part of the Sociology/Anthropology Department's small but growing collection of stones and bones.

LUCY

It's 4 a.m. in Willis, I
Thought I was all alone. I
Look up in the darkness.
There she was, no hair, no

Skin. Just pieces of her
Bones. Her name is
Lucy she is old, so old
She is so old she is
Petrified.
But Lucy can't tell us her
Story? Because
She is 3.18 million
YEARS OLD

Later, the talented Randy designed a Kuchina-type sculpture made of recycled material to be placed in the Weitz Center. Recycling is one of Randy's strong values.

Spencer Reece was our nationally-published poet, the one with the scarf. He's now an Episcopal priest. Spencer's *Road to Emmaus* was nominated in 2014 for a National Book Award for poetry. When he came back to town for the first time and read his poetry in the Atheneum he was greatly moved as he talked about his Northfield life and still carried that love with him on his later reading from *The Road to Emmaus*, hosted by Doug and Ruth Crane. After writing here, Spencer began working at Brooks Brothers in the Mall of America and wrote his *New Yorker* poem, *The Clerk*. It's crazy, but now we think of Spencer everyday when we drive north on Linden Street. When he lived here, Spencer had a special hangout at a Kinko-like shop with Karen, whom he called "Special K." Karen said he was someone you'd just like to take home with you. And Martha and Robert Arthur, hoped to do just that, saving him a place next to theirs in the cemetery in Valley Grove.

There were poems about Valley Grove: the poet Bob Tisdale's "Graveyard in Valley Grove: Dusk Before Memorial Day."

He says he's been in Vietnam,
he's damned if he'll be buried here,
no, not with the other dead men of the family.

CARLETON SECURITY BLOTTER, May 12, 10:50 am. Security was notified that the Northfield Police had taken a theft report from the owner of a large, expensive fiberglass horse that had apparently been stolen from their property.

Everything all screwed up—
no, let me be buried far off,
so only God and I know where.

"I won't lock it," he says to me.
"I'll leave the gate open for you."
I hear as I climb the hill to find my son.
Shadows lengthening in the churchyard,
and the two white buildings bare
beneath the skullcap of the sky.

I tell him what I heard—
a Gothic photograph of needy
solitude and darkness. And when
we leave the yard and close the gate,
I see it has no lock.

Poetry was everywhere. Norman Butler brought us Poetry and a Pint for special nights at his Contented Cow Pub, and there were nights held there for discussion groups, Beers and Brains? It was a great day when Norman Butler and Diane Burry came to town. They started everything—our first Indian restaurant on Division Street, our first Northfield pub, the Contented Cow (named by Barbara Burke) with live music, as well as many other restaurants we loved and missed. Norm was wise in every way, and was once quoted as saying: "If the world was emptied of all but North and Field, North would quarrel with Field, and Field with North." We should write a book about all the Northfield arguments—the misunderstandings between the glitterati and the literati, architecture for St. Dominic, fighting farewells to the Grain Elevator and its Christmas tree. We longed for even more great English people to spark up our lives, maybe even the way we speak. (But if you phone Chapati, we think it's Norm's voice trying to pretend he's Indian.) Some Englishmen came and some left through the years, but Jim McDonnell (more Irish, really), Barbara and Jonathan Hill stayed. Keith Harrison, although Australian, not English, brightened up Northfield along with his Swedish wife, Christina, and two red-haired daughters, gave us our first splash of poetry, bringing old friends from the Iowa Writer's Workshop, tips on the stock market, and on some occasions, even the didgeridoo. And then came the Africans. It seemed to almost happen in one exciting year. There was Kofi Owusu and Bereket Haileab. Cherif Keita, originally from Mali, took a position in the French Department, following a set of coincidences, which often seems what Cherif's life was all about. Later came his wife Maimouna Toure, who, in the early years, magically transformed our landscape with colorful African dresses and brought family members here who kept it up. Cherif brought Francophone Studies combined with joyous greetings to Carleton and its town. There were excited waves and ça va's that sustained us every day and we became for a few warming moments his old and new best friend. Little did Cherif or Northfield know that his life and work, by another set of coincidences would be connected by amazing discoveries.

Cherif had begun a study of missionaries in South Africa, and became interested in William Wilcox and his wife Isabella Clary Wilcox. In the middle of the night while reading a biography of Wilcox, Cherif found out that William and his wife Idabella had been married in Northfield, Minnesota. He began pacing the floor, not daring for a long time to look at the book again. The Wilcoxes had adopted John Dube, a young African man and brought him to America. Dube later became the founder of the African National Congress, previous to Nelson Mandela. Later, after finding the descendants of the Wilcox family, Cherif investigated Idabella's Northfield roots. He found the four Clary graves right behind his house on Marvin Lane in the Northfield Cemetery; Cherif's son and his Boy Scout friend cleaned the graves and repaired the broken crown on the gravestone in preparation for a visit from the Wilcox descendants. From these discoveries came three films: *Cemetery Stories: A Rebel Missionary in South Africa, Oberlin-Inanda: The Life And Times Of John L Dube*, who was the founder of the Ohlange Institute near Verulam, the first editor of the Ilanga Lase Natal, the isiZulu newspaper, and the first president of the Native Congress, forerunner to the African National Congress and *Remembering Nokutela Mdima Dube—Africa is a Country.*

POLICE LOG, May 29. An officer assisted the State Patrol with a very large snapping turtle in a traffic lane along Highway 19.

MEETING NORTHFIELDERS

O F COURSE MOST PEOPLE ARE KNOWN NOT BY THEIR ART BUT BY their coats or their cars, and the cars used to honk at us, saying hello. Now with those short honks when everyone enters their cars, it drives us crazy, thinking it's asking us to wave. Just for fun, you might start making friends by checking out their clothes or their hairdos. Remember, people with orange or turquoise hair need attention, be sure to say "Hi" to men with ponytails, and try to get to know people with rings in their nose. And if you're a little scared, there are great taming rituals. Saying "Good Morning" when passing in the park will protect you (Remember Maya Angelou's poem: "Say simply, very simply, with hope, Good Morning.") Two genius winners summered on Nevada Street, and when one was asked how he had changed, it turned out that he had started saying "Good Morning" to people. We had yet another mad genius on Winona Street, our most wildly creative artist, whose hair resembled Einstein's. David Lefkowitz, with fellow Northfield artist Doug Bratland, created *Nirthfolde*, a bucolic, yet bustling burg situated in a parallel universe, occupying temporarily the premises of the Northfield Arts Guild. The installation included misinformation panels, ahistorical artifacts and other mildly perplexing displays: a misleading map and information about the Cowling Arboretum Transit System and a scale model of a prehistoric beaver lodge metropolis. Other Lefkowitz creations include a wall of styrofoam packing material arranged to re-

semble a model of an urban metropolis, giant drawings *on* flattened cor-
rugated boxes *of* architectural follies made entirely of cardboard boxes,
and, in collaboration with art deptartment colleague Stephen Mohring,
18 Holes in One, a mini-golf hole playable at the Walker Art Center's
sculpture garden.

Still, you maybe shouldn't start staying "Good Night" in the park, but
admiring a necklace is a sure way to start a conversation. Still you'll have
questions. Here's the thing. There's a society here, and you may need to
break into it or start your own. But remember this, we love new people;
we're a little tired of each other. We'll eat you up!

LIVING SAFELY IN OUR TOWN

So if you're saying "Good Morning" to everyone, you may wonder if
the town is safe. Billi Bergh reminded us that it's a small world so you'd
better behave. And for your personal safety, don't refuse to play Alphonse
and Gaston at four-way stops. Always be careful or you might end up
with Cindy, that once famous ER nurse, who said she loved to tear into a
pair of Calvin Kleins. You may even wonder whether you might need a
burglar alarm. Several years ago a Marketing Intern came to Northfield.
He told us that there were a lot of houses going up farther down the
block and he felt that all of us should know about protecting our homes.
He said he would give us a free Honeywell burglar alarm system, and a
sign for our yard. This incident became known as The Marketing Intern
and the Philosophers. The first neighbor told him that this was against
our philosophy, and he said, "What philosophy?" She waved her arms,
made happy circles in the air, and said, "Complete Trust." Later when
he called on Shouri Daniels at 320 Union, he was told that having an
alarm was against her philosophy. He said what philosophy? And she
said: "Spirituality" He asked, "What spirituality? And she said, "Chinese." However, those with philosophers with complete trust and spirituality and the Open Door philosophy are open to surprises. Molly's
needlepoint welcome "Come on In" sign she used for parties, if left at
the door, sometimes invited perfect strangers inside. And there was that
sweet house, home of the bowmaker on West Second Street, that after a
hard winter had a greeting in colored chalk on the sidewalk: "Happiness
is Here"—certainly an invitation to walk in and explore. Barbara and

Hartley had someone walk in and sit beside them in their living room while they were watching television. When the police came to find him, he said: "Isn't this Owatonna?" A well-dressed matron stopped by and asked Lydia's housepainter, one Jim McCorkell (who when he stopped painting, grew up to be the founder of College Possible) if she could please come in. She knew there was a treasure in the basement and she was prepared to dig for it. And when Toni came downstairs in the middle of the night there was a little guy in pajamas sleeping on her couch. Don't worry too much about these incidents. Northfield was among the top twenty-one safest cities chosen by Safe Choice Security. But come on, why were Lakeville and Farmington seven and three? It was probably because those more backward towns had so few philosophers and not as much hospitality.

Victor and Kiffi had the most exciting adventure with Northfield hospitality. On one hot and humid July night they were comforted only by a huge ceiling fan over their bed, although they kept waking up fitfully, then slipping back into semi-consciousness, that feeling when it's almost too hot to breathe. Victor was lying awake, listening to a heavy rasping noise, feeling sympathy for Kiffi with her allergies, breathing so heavily, when Kiffi says *out loud* to him: "Victor, what's that terrible breathing noise?"

Panic, then he says: "I thought it was you." Kiffi thought maybe it was a raccoon that had come down the chimney. Victor thought it sounded like a big old dog breathing heavily, and suggested that she slide out on his side of bed, go out the bedroom door and get the big flashlight in his office. Victor would then go out in the hall and hold the bedroom door shut so that the "raccoon" or "big dog" wouldn't get into the rest of the house. Kiffi got the flashlight, Victor cautiously opened the bedroom door, kneeled down, scanned the flashlight under the bed, and was thunderstruck (is there a stronger word?) when the light came full upon the face of a man, lying on the floor sleeping on Kiffi's side of the bed, snoring heavily.

POLICE LOG, June 5. Police investigated a complaint of indecent exposure after a young child was urinating in public in the 1500 block of Koester Court. The father of the child was "advised that this was not a good idea."

Without telling what he had seen, Victor stood up, calmly closed the door and said, in an "un-Victorish" calm tone: "Kiffi, please go downstairs and call 911. I'll be there by the time you get them."

"Aren't you even going to tell me what you saw?" she said in a loud irritated voice. Victor, in exaggerated calm repeated his request and added, "Please call them NOW!" She went grumpily downstairs, called 911, and about the time the police had asked her what her mother's maiden name was, and then "What's the problem?" Kiffi looked up at Victor and said:

"What do I tell them is the problem?"

"Tell them there is a man sleeping on the floor next to our bed." Then Victor said, to the speechless Kiffi: "*Tell them* there is a man sleeping on the floor next to our bed."

When 911 told them to leave the house, go outside, and wait for the police to come, Kiffi hesitated, saying she was not about to go out on the street in her nightgown. Victor later said while he was sleeping he had wondered if a bat had flown into the ceiling fan and brushed his leg, and Kiffi felt that someone was trying to pull the sheet tighter on her side.

Later after the police arrived and dragged the guy out of the house, Kiffi and Victor looked around and saw that there had been more than one person, that the other bedrooms had mussed sheets and head-dented pillows, and one had thoughtfully taken off his shoes outside the back door and left them there. Later the police chief reported that the sleepy men were drunk and had been in three "philosophers" houses on the block to sleep that night.

NORTHFIELD'S MEDICAL FACILITIES

You'll also need to know about doctors, and where to go. We have good medical care in Northfield, with many choices. We felt quite modern when we had an internist named Tiffany, but she disappeared. We've got a fairly new hospital now in Turbine Territory. When hospital treatment rooms were smaller, a group of great, courageous gal pals were told to quiet down in the waiting room, but they just laughed and answered: "We're special, we're terminal."

With the exception of the exceptional Dr. Mark Mellstrom, our then-doctors with those small practices are no longer with us, or have left us to go fly fishing in exotic places. Our dentists go deer hunting and leave the place to the dental hygienists, who are then tempted to go wild and play the music they like just a little bit louder. It's the hygienists we're devoted to. Thanks to their preventive help and the free toothbrushes and those proxa brushes we haven't seen our dentists above the waist for years. We choose dentists if we go for their hygienists. There was the luscious Laurie followed by the fascinating Judy. Sam Harris (not a Northfielder but someone who writes about atheism) has confessed that even he sometimes feels a spiritual rapture at his desk or while he gets his teeth cleaned.) Laurie revealed that for little old ladies, a trip to the hygienist became a special occasion and they often dressed up for it.

We had Family Health, Women's Health, and Allina. Allina had an art gallery, with many exhibits we often missed due to our darn good health. There was a new exhibit every few weeks. Leslie's photograph "Garden of Quiet Listening" that remained at the far end of the lab helped to lower our blood pressure.

Allina used to give "baseball" cards out for all of their doctors. We loved trading, and we'd give three of our cards for one of Dr. Ehresmann, our first woman doctor, and three for one of Dr. Saul, our much-loved obstetrician/gynecologist, who had a very nice picture. At first the cards were giant, too big to put in your pocket, but now they're like business cards with photos. They're still a comfort for schoolchildren who could play a game like Authors with them in the waiting room. They could look at the back of the card and read their histories, then try to guess who they were. If you want to look further, there are large photos near the entrance with larger photos of each doctor (at a comfortable height for nurses and their kids to play Pin the Tail on the Donkey after hours.) Since all the doctors are good, you could choose the one you wanted or just see how many the family could go through in a year. Still, our favorite was Doctor NESNA. Smiles were good. It turns out that 80% of winning political candidates are good at smiling. We liked the smiling, welcoming ones dressed in scrubs, ready for action. It's like those presidential portraits in the Larson Room at the Weitz Center. Howard Swearer, surrounded by his compatriots in robes and suits is the only one in a shirt ready to roll up his sleeves, not just posing, but ready to get to work.

Family Health, located on the Hospital grounds, didn't have baseball cards but a photo of one of their popular physicians used to pop up as a big surprise on the internet when we were reading our email. We miss it now. Of course many of us stopped and finally refused to email. Once when we asked our good friend David if he did email, he said, no, he did Haldol.

MAKING FRIENDS IN NORTHFIELD

But you'll probably have smaller concerns—about what you should wear, or how to avoid time-slurping friendships or entangling alliances.

So many women were "on their life journey" that it seemed no one was home. The rest of them were leaning in and were too busy trying to turn that journey into a trajectory.

Be a little suspicious of other "foreigners." Those southern women could say the worst things about each other if they remembered to start with the words "Bless her heart." (And if you, too, are a southern woman, take off those pastel suits; they look stupid in the snow, and you're not having lunch with Nancy Pelosi.)

And you, you being young, may even speak Uptalk, that kind of speaking that sounds like you are eternally asking questions. But don't worry about acceptance. Upskirting was a definite no-no, but Uptalk was fine. Even Terry Gross does it on *Fresh Air*. Beginning with Seven Up, everything became Up, especially the changing bids on that Tiger Trail. And there was now Upshot and Upworthy, Uptick, and the shivery Updraft.

And now for our homegrown. If you say something outrageous or shocking to our Minnesotans, their only answer will be "That's different." Or they may ask if you want to "come with," while you sit waiting around for the "me" or "us." We talk as if we've taken speech lessons from Governor Dayton. Gawker had an Ugly Accent Contest for cities recently and Minneapolis was seeded as coming in seventh. And so many Minnesotans looked seriously serious. Now there's an app for that (not really), but new research suggests that it is possible to treat depression (or maybe just serious faces) by paralyzing key facial muscles with Bo-

||||||||||||||||||||||||||||||||||||||||||||||||||||||||||||||||||||||||||||||||||||||||||||||||||||||||||||||||||||||||||||||||||||||||||

POLICE LOG, June 24. Animal Complaint. A caller in the sub-100 block of Viking Terrace reported that a dog was barking and yipping. An officer arrived and found that a chicken was actually making the noise. The chicken calmed down while the officer was present.

tox, which prevents people from frowning and having unhappy-looking faces. It's like the reverse of crying when you're really not sad but crying can make you sad, just as Henry James once said: "We do not cry because we're sad. We're sad because we cry." Minnesota seemed to be the only state where fun was more an adjective than a noun. And now that we're old Minnesotans, we don't want to be called "dear" and we hate baby talk. But what will you call us: Girls? Ladies? Women? Gals? There's really no good answer, but you could just try "Young Lady," and duck. And by the way, if you're of the masculine brand, and someone calls you Sir — it's not exactly respect, it's impatience.

But in this society, you'll still come across some Antique Mean Girls, and others young enough to think good manners are for frightened sissies. And the friendly ones you yearned for seem to have lost many rich opportunities to shut up. Some Northfielders when asked if they ever lied, said, "Whenever we have to. We call it manners." They didn't gossip, but they did do what they called social history. And you must watch out when you're gossiping about people in Northfield, especially old Northfielders, all of whom seem to be related to each other. The Lambertys were related by blood and through marriages to the Estrems, Ottes, Quinnells, Schuettes, Fesslers, and the Johnsons of Dennison. The Storlies were related to the Grisims, and the Grisims were related to the Pasches. The Legvolds were related to the Larsons and the Harknesses were related to the Ayottes.

There might always be a problem of fitting in, but there are endless ways of figuring it out in Northfield. You could fly an American flag for every patriotic holiday and get a Norwegian mailbox, or get a plaque giving the date your house was built but only if it was before 1900. You could join two book clubs or start your own. You could start your own vegetable garden in your front yard, use its products to make healthy vegetarian meals, compost the leftovers or freeze your garbage, never go to Target or Cub, join every protest, sign petitions, never use plastic, never shop on Amazon, hide your television, throw away that plastic bag and carry a great-looking basket to the Farmer's Market. (You could ask Linda Morral to bring you one from Nantucket.)

Still, there were goody-goodies who were truly good. Living together here, arriving at the same time, having babies together, can build lasting friendships. We'll always remember A, B, C, D: Ann, Betsy, Charlotte and Deane, Northfield friends forever. Still, don't fall completely for that Minnesota Nice thing. (We're not all from here.) If you want to be proud, think about the more distinctive Minnesota Mouth, a way of dentistry taught at the U of M so that dentists from every other state will know where you're from or where you've been whenever you open your mouth. And when they open their mouths, you should be aware that some Northfielders were known for certain words. Even if they've left town, it seems as if they still own them. Sophie's was "Incredible," and Ellen's trademark word was "Absolutely." Leah started many sentences with "To be honest." Ruth's was "Diety." And Ruthie loved the word "Cozy." Judy owned "I love it." Sandra had captured "But that's just me." The word "And" belonged to Barbara, but you could feel free to use it to start a sentence if you didn't get too excited when you said it. Yes, words can be owned. Not long ago there was a lawsuit about Who owned How? Chobani Yogurt "stole" How from an advertising company who had also used it in a book of the same name called *How*.

However, we were humbled when it came to language. Brenda stood in front of her bathroom mirror, opening her mouth wide, trying to say "Awesome." Babette would go deep in thought, say "I'm," and struggle to add the word "like" before finishing the sentence. Loretta, although she kept looking at her watch, tried to "hang out."

NORTHFIELD VALUES

You should know that we don't enjoy pretension in our wonderful town. When Russ announced that he made Eggs Benedict for Christmas breakfast, Barbara said: "Oh, yes, like Egg McMuffins." In Northfield, we go out for breakfast, not Brunch. And what about those Northfield children wearing a little green t-shirt that said: *I read 1000 books before kindergarten* that they got at our library?

POLICE LOG, *July 4. An officer advised a person on how to get two purses out of a tree that were used to get a shoe unstuck from the tree at Central Park.*

Our lips were sealed when Northfield Yarn had a knitting session for Yale alumni. And when our children (who may have finally read 1000 books) came back to town they were surprised that Northfield was so pretentious as to name a Division Street store Agora. And later they'd say, "Oh, Mom, we always hoped for an Oil and Vinegar store, and now we have one!"

If you have a Lexus, watch out. (Lexus is really just a made-up name, putting together luxury and technology and charging a lot.) Just remember, Pope Francis gave up his papal chariot for a Ford Focus. (Ford once asked the poet Marianne Moore to name some new cars, and she chose Mongoose Civique, Utopian Turtletop, and Pastelogram. And after these suggestions, the Edsel was born.) Owners with other luxury cars could hide them from the unaware by highlighting the word Sears near the rear license. In the winter when it's really cold, watch out for women wearing faux faux furs. And if you're asked if you might be a proud owner of a Toto, say "no no."

And there was the Carleton Rec Center, which Jim, Sid, and Perry (mountaineers, runners and sailors) called the Taj, preferring to stay in their own Calcutta in the stadium. But you can learn to love the Rec Center for its extra benefits. There's Mikki Showers, the director, born to be there. Motorcycling Mikki started out in the Business Office but later made the Rec Center a home away from home. There are the personal trainers — Kitty Runzheimer, who taught all the older "athletes" except for the ones that were seeking trainers who resembled their granddaughters. There was Thad Caron, who also ran that tough Boot Camp for employees, and Jenna Kuhlman. Her grateful client Barbara Jenkins told Jenna that she looked like Vermeer's "Girl with the Pearl Earring," and now she wears one. Where else could you see two future college presidents racing on twin treadmills, or two guys rowing together on twin boats. The stadium had an outdoor track, but the Rec Center had its own outside runway. And there were special guests who'd come back to town to exercise as family members — puzzling sights such as Alison Easter (dancer and personal trainer) rapidly walking backwards on the treadmill, as usual knowing something we don't know. The covered runway

I'm so Northfield I think snow should never melt till April. — CGF

was the pathway to the Rec Center entrance, and a good way to check out people from inside when on your personal ellipsis. So if you're new to walking on the runway or an ectomorph messing with mesomorphs, hold shoulders back, suck it in, walk or run fast, and in winter, pretend you're not cold. There is an outer runway for nature lovers—arbwalkers, walking groups. There are the women walkers, who meet in the mornings at Blue Monday (and everyone seemed to wish they were part of it) and come walking fast with Leona Openshaw in a cute baseball cap, heading the pack, and there are women bikers all in yellow or lime green t-shirts. There was Molly's group, bravely facing wind and winter, and mystery people accompanied by dogs. In certain seasons we could relive the drama of college life—students with suitcases and laundry, walking by overloaded, especially with helpful parents. There was the grass runway in between where you could watch bunnies running faster than you.

FINDING FINAL FRIENDS

And did you come here looking for a new partner? This is something we need to organize. Some of our happily marrieds should share their secrets, especially the ones who knew how to stop all their arguments by singing the Oscar Meyer Weiner song. Some second marriages seemed to just be cultural exchanges. But a few women have come here to find the love of their life. Fortunately, that's usually once again a second marriage, with not quite so much of life to go, where they've already been over the bumps. You might try the dog park and meet some friendly single pet parents, although you might be known for a long time only by your dog's name. Why not re-name your dog as a form of self-expression, if not self-advertising—maybe Cognoscenti to show you have an imagination, or Spot, to show you're just a good-time gal, in no way snobby. If you don't already have one, try to get a really cute dog. As you probably know, people often look like their dogs. A Swiss study says it's also possible to match people with their cars, because they look alike. Researchers took car photos from various angles, as well as photos of the owners' faces. Then they gave strangers six photographs of faces and asked them to choose which one went with a certain car. They ranked them from the most likely owner to the least likely. If it was a side or rear view of the car, they couldn't do it, but when they looked at the front of the car, the scores went up dramatically. Looking at cars from the front, we see faces: windshields are the forehead, headlights are eyes. (In fact, David Flanagan was on top of it when he designed big eyelashes for the headlights of his Italian neighbor's Volkswagen.) Side-view mirrors are ears, and the grills can be noses or even a mouth. Because of these front-end designs you can give personality traits to cars. We all know that the VW Beetle is happy, but we might not have been aware that the Honda Civic was accused of having a "neurotic" appearance, and the BMW 645ci had a dominant (that's for sure) and angry scowl.

Those who had met a new partner through Christian Mingle seem to expect permanence since God had chosen for them. What does mingle mean anyway? (But so you don't get mixed up, Sparks, its parent company also owns JDate, BlackSingles and, for older romantics, SilverSingles.) But just for you, who keep up with things, we now have Gluten Free Singles. And what's up with this soul mate thing? For some of us, men were now a foreign country. New research on rodents left alone in a room with a male scientist or his t-shirt caused a sharp and massive spike in their stress hormones. These rodents showed no such reaction to females. Most of our famous Northfield feminists are now believed to have divorced or gone to law school or became grandmothers. In later years, you-know-what finally became hilarious. And Gloria Steinem (although no biologist) said that with a thin and undemanding libido, new cells could be released for creativity. Lois Lowry, who wrote *The Giver*, said that these hormonal changes made a woman want to plant delphiniums.

We could be happy with pretend husbands: As a rule, many of the good ones were named Pete. There was also Jeff Deuth, the Sammon brothers from Faribault, Gordie Michelson, John Tripp, Bernie Street, Bill Hunt (who'd come in the middle of the night if the furnace broke and is now remembered by Hunt Cottage on Union Street) Tom and Jim of T and J from Faribault, Pete Carlson, Peter Lee, Mark Ekeren, all the Keith Pumper Guys. All Vintage Men. Sometimes the real husbands hid when these Alpha Dogs rang the doorbell. (Okay, some were border collies, not Alpha dogs.) House husbands liked their company. When they came, we thought of much more work that needed to be done. And they smiled and pretended that they weren't talking with someone who knew nothing. And let us praise Mr. Claude O'Neill, a true artist, who was too busy to be a complete pretend husband, but who restored and saved the historic floors of both Northfield and Grand Marais.

And the real now-husbands at times knew more (although not more than the pretend husbands) than their real wives. Then the computer came along and the real wives found out that sometimes they knew more than the real husbands because suddenly they could divide the brain into different jobs. Those husbands had great registry and perfect storage. And some wives had better retrieval and speed. These wives then held their heads up high and were no longer afraid of superiority storms. And some of our women became more famous than men. Peggy Prowe had a *bridge* named after her. That beats the Taco Bell Professor of Spanish Literature. For a while when we didn't know what was up, we called it the "Bridge to Nowhere?" Peggy, by the way, had also discovered the word "Parenting" before anyone used it, and did all she could so that we could bike on a trail from Northfield to Faribault and finally to Owatonna. (Maybe she could give that man at the Hartley Clarks a ride.)

But then with computers, the equality machines, came Virtual Husbands! Those old high school boyfriends or wannabeen boyfriends, who suddenly found us and wondered what we looked like after all those years. No problem, no pictures. But we had memories, innocent flirtations, philosophical discussions about aging. And we could easily switch virtual boyfriends, or get a lot of them, going from elove to eeeeelove. Some were known to visit those virtual husbands, even with their real husbands tagging along.

MORE SCARY TECHNOLOGY

Our college students didn't need computers, since they always had their phones. At first the cellphones were hidden in their pockets, but later they walked along just looking at them or talking to them and smiling. They'll never walk alone. Morgan Light, class of 2017 at the School of Visual Arts, finally designed a helmet that holds the cellphone in front of your face, since she knew no one could happily put them down. It wasn't true that students wanted to be alone with their phones; they

||||||||||||||||||||||||||||||||||||||||||||||||||||||||||||||||||||||||||||||||||||||||||||||||||||||||||||||||||||||||||

POLICE LOG, July 5. Vandalism. A curb was coated with wax at Sibley Elementary School.

also wanted to be together with their phones. The cellphones were great for mental health, making it quite possible to talk to yourself as loud as you want and still be blue-tooth normal. And cellphone conversations overheard could turn us into minor playwrights, joining the drama, hearing one side of the cellphone conversations and trying to write the script for the other part. Sometimes we like to write an email, and end it with "sent from my thighbone." And Ben Lundeen would write: "Sent from my WWII crystal radio set." In the beginning it was all new to us. Later, we felt sorry because we had no iPad until we saw a woman who had no iPhone. We had been phone pioneers, happy to witness this final development. Many years ago when AT and T split up we got new phones, including pink Princess ones and when they rang they sounded like birds, so we never answered. And then the birds outside started sounding like phones, and we ran into our houses.

After that we got voice mail. Rick liked to answer the phone pretending he was the machine. Dixon Bond's voice mail said: "This is Bond. Dixon Bond." Later Robbie the Robot starting answering everyone's phones, and he was some boring man who made us forget the number we dialed. After that we worked on our phone to fix it up and get rid of the robot. But sometimes then the phone would start yelling in Spanish. When Shouri tried to call her family in India, she often got the police.

Women at home were protected by their husband's name listed in the phone book, even when their husbands were no longer there. And then, later, women could have their name right there by their husband's, but it cost extra money to do that, just as it cost extra money to stay with their husbands.

We were always being advised to buy phones for our bathroom, which seemed like a very silly marketing idea. But then phones became portable. We were tempted to get even with our friends who washed dishes when talking, calling them from our bathroom, a guilty but satisfying secret. *Consumer Reports* now tells us that we can Run Our Home from our Phone, instead of just running our phone from our home.

Toni was the first person in town to get a portable phone. But everything got mixed up and she was receiving all of the phone calls meant for Molly, Northfield's epicenter, as well as her own, bringing back the historic party line.

Now you, too, Tyvek Towners, are going to need a phone. If you're stuck with a landline, you're best to get 645s. Our favorite numbers began with 645. Six-four-five meant that you were trustworthy—that you had been here a long time and hadn't been run out of town. Later, some upstarts were able to sneak in with a 645, after someone died. And after that, everyone decided that 663 was the New Northfield. And then 301 got it.

ANALYZING NORTHFIELD SOCIETY

Sometimes the *Northfield News* will help you get tips for analyzing society. Our early help was a *Northfield News* article by LaVern Rippley, west side professor and east side landowner:

> Periodically western societies engage in class warfare. The classic example from our time is by Karl Marx in his Community Manifesto.
>
> Class warfare is more than military, more than economics. Sometimes it takes the shape of latent racism, religious bigotry, or aristocrats vs. the polloi.
>
> Northfield's rental ordinance-in-the making is turning into Marxist-Cromwellian, Postvillian class warfare.
>
> No open street brawls, no physical injury yet but plenty of hurt. Mass legislation is proposed to blanket our whole region to skirt a local scene of class warfare—guillotining members of all three estates—lords, clergy and peasants. Badly needed in the proposal though absent from the approach thus far is a dash of ordinary common sense.
>
> Hence, my proposal: Acknowledge that Northfield's class warfare can be confined to a local region—the East Side Neighborhood. Unlike the class warfare of medieval Europe, this one is different. Here the first estate is comprised not of kings but of the moment elite of the east side neighborhood. The second

---

I'm so Northfield I remember when some of my friends still had party lines. And not the 976 kind. — Chris Forbes

I'm so Northfield I remember when we only had to dial 5 digits to call anyone in town 5-1234. — Lori Farmer

estate is best labeled not as scholarly monks but as members of the fifth finest college in the nation, perhaps in the world. The third estate more accurately delineated this time is comprised of the intellectually gifted students at that highly endowed and richly acclaimed Fifth best. Thus for the first time in history we have elites of whom the first is striving to cannibalize the other two. Let's not waste our time legislating for all of Northfield. Let's cut to the chase with a solution.

Best we first rename the district, calling it the "Third Ward," that section of the city from 12 to 3 o'clock extending indefinitely eastward on Woodley and northward along the Cannon River, then crossing to move up Highway 3. Popularly, the moniker for this would be the Third Rike, especially because it would rhyme with "bike" because an issue equally as offensive as the students is affecting Fourth Street. Our mini-nation might be also called Bike Rike. Here we could control the renters, these third estate, these learned but "homeless" commoners we call college students. We would need to call in Albert Speareful to redesign the old middle school into a fine arts exhibit hall where we could display and dispose of immoral art and similar clutter. Needless to say, the feudalistic Mietskaserene at Fourth and Washington east of Union would be replaced by villas, Berlina-Dahlem style. Patrolling this Third Reich would be the building inspection division known as Gestalpo, named for the dog food, hounding out commoners who congregated in numbers larger than three per unit. Day and night, armed with wolf jackets and in an array of weapons including DNA needles to get samples, they would bang on doors, snoop through premises and verify relationships in affordable housing units. While this were going on, a conference would be called for East Seventh at the Winnersee swimming pool headed by Reinhard Heidenreich, assigned the task of devising a final solution to the rental problems of the Bike Rike.

Because all of this would take perhaps up to 12 years, however, I propose within a 10-year time to turn the entire Third into paradise, density dormitory style—and suddenly with Snow White and her dwarfs, the "East Side Neighborhood" will rest in peace.

For, then, the entire Third will be run by its new order, the SS ... "Superior Students."

(This author had a fine background for the article, having written a book called *Of German Ways*.)

Then came the Big Reveal. In 2014 LaVern Rippley, in a Valentine's Day surprise for the superior students and administrators in the fifth best college, donated their two most interesting homes on East Second Street to St. Olaf College: "LaVern Rippley Donates Love, Crack to Olaf" (*The Carletonian*, February 14th, 2014) Now what if Rippley in the future donated all his east side houses to St. Olaf to be used as spy compounds, so St. Olaf could spy on Carleton? However, presently, LaVern Rippley still takes good care of these two famous houses, somewhat easier now that the students are gone.

TROLLING FOR NEWS

Writing like LaVern's was one of the highlights of the *Northfield News*. Where else can you learn what's really going on?

How do you ever keep up with things? Our Ladies from Lonsdale were information sherpas, passing the word that someone was building a new garage and might be finding a new wife. The Grand Theatre, now an Event Center, announced weddings: "Alex and Anna From Here to Eternity," "I do. Me, too. Savannah and John. Let's Party," "New Year/New Life/Kyle and Kelly," "Happily Ever After, Kimberly and Kristopher," "Christine and Chris Forever," "Tying the Knot Starring Nicole and Erik," "We've Got Chemistry Heather and Kyle," "Together in Mutual Weirdness, Zach & Arie Forever," and more mysterious marquee notices, such as: "Ron and Car 70-70-50." Was Ron celebrating his car? Was it made 70 years ago, in 1944 and now is Ron 70 and has had it for 50 years, buying it used in 1964? There was the Wayne Eddy Affair on the radio, interviewing prominent citizens. Of course there might be too much news. When the *Northfield News* started having two issues per week, a few people wanted to cancel their subscription but the *Northfield News* said No! No! No! Around that time, Jack Tripp applied in person to be a proofreader at the *News*. And they told Jack, "We don't have a

|||||||||||||||||||||||||||||||||||||||||||||||||||||||||||||||||||||||||||||||||||||||||||||||||||||||||||||||||||||||||||||||||||||||||||

I'm so Northfield I saw Rocky Horror Picture Show at The Grand when it was still a movie theater. — Heather Murphy Capps

proofreader," to which Jack replied, "I know it." Something's changed since then and there are few mistakes.

Our favorite writer to the *Northfield News* gave a shout-out to his compatriots: "Journalism professors say that the best letters are the shortest. They also say that the letters to the editor are the most read part of a newspaper—more than the sports, the comics or the crossword. I smell a Pulitzer Prize. Arthur Paul David White."

On June 4, 2014, one issue of the *Northfield News* on page 6A seemed determined to go national—giving a whole page to updated reports on Lindsay Lohan and Detroit. Save your copy if you have one. It might be valuable like those stamps that had been printed upside down. You could get some news by joining a book club, but the news could be a month old; still, who cares in a small town? Sometimes it takes a while to pile up stuff, but if you stick around long enough you can find out who has the flu or whose daughter tragically married into the wrong political party—with the only clue so far a lapel flag pin worn by both parents. You could read all those great posters in the entrance of Blue Monday, the Northfield Arts Guild, or the Northfield Library. Then there were the college sites like carlslist, where you could speculate on others by what they sold or what they wanted. Some people were giving away so many things, you might be afraid they were going to jump off the roof.

POLICE LOG, *July 6. Road Hazard. Somebody placed a large flowerpot in the road in the 1600 block of Highway 19.*

NORTHFIELD SPIRITUAL LIFE

O F COURSE YOU'LL NEED TO KNOW WHAT FORM OF SPIRITUAL OR religious life is right for you, and you're in a perfect place to do it. Arthur Paul David White, in a letter to the *Northfield News*, let us know that Jeane Dixon had written, years ago, that "by the year 2000, Northfield Minnesota, would be a spiritual center rivaling the Vatican." (Pre-Googleable)

We admired our Pied Pipers—the pastors, reverends, ministers, priests, and rabbis—so much that we feared that they'd be called away and replaced by moppets.

If you first enter our town on Highway 23, Bethel, with its movie marquee on the left, would be first to welcome you: "You Are Welcome Here."

Churches are perhaps the very best places to meet your Northfielders, for solace, for community, for coffee or soup, and for feelings of security.

Other than the marquee, the churches' best weapons were their bells and they didn't use them enough. There was the 9:30AM bell on summer Sundays, to make you feel guilty in your robe. And St. Dominic's old 7PM bells for mass each evening, that were often quite musical. But nothing felt more exhilarating than walking to church when the bells were ringing. Some folks would say, "Why do we need church when we have Starbucks and yoga?" All of this reminds us of overhearing a woman say: "We're Catholics, we're covered," in response to a small uproar. (And now with Pope Francis, they may be). Others went from the Baptist church to the Buddhists to massage and acupuncture. Or others would go to the Buddhists first thing in the morning, then take a shower and join the Episcopalians. Ecumenicism was a kick.

Many years ago, Amy Gage wrote about the BUDDHIST MEDITATION CENTER in the *Minneapolis Star Tribune*: "Three guys and a buddha" got together in Northfield in 1996 and sowed the seeds for what is now the Northfield Buddhist Meditation Center—a plain, handsome room above a jewelry store, 313½ Division Street. At that time Ted Tuel, an ordained lay Buddhist, said that "Mindfulness" was a key: "That means being fully involved in what you are doing. The moment is all we have. Fully engage in a task and make it new. You may change your relationship to the World." At that time Amy noted that the Buddhist Meditation Center was just down the hall from the Quaker meeting, the Center for Sustainable Living, People for Peace and Goodwill, and the Fellowship of Reconciliation. So Northfield! The Center supports meditation practice and spiritual development of its members by offering dharma talks, classes, practice groups, retreats, a library, and daily meditation sits, all offered in the spirit of *Dana*, generosity, paid by voluntary contributions.

The NORTHFIELD EVANGELICAL FREE CHURCH may become the newest church for serving Tyvek Town, nested in a lovely suburban setting, extremely inviting and looking as if it truly belongs there. Pastor Daniel Runke wants all to know that the mission of the Evangelical Free Church is to develop an authentic commitment to following Jesus Christ by serving in the church, community, and the world. The church seeks to do that by making Jesus Christ the Center of all they do.

ALL SAINTS EPISCOPAL CHURCH is the oldest church in Northfield. They began praying in 1852, became incorporated earlier in 1858, the same year, 1858, that Minnesota became a state. All Saints has had a longstanding presence along Washington Street at the edge of downtown since then. The Prairie Gothic structure, one of many consecrated by Bishop Henry Whipple, has been the subject of undergraduate art history papers—one by Terry Pfoutz, former church member, among them. This exquisite small church, blessed with stained glass windows honoring historic Northfielders, has recently expanded, and the new church is well-deserved and truly exciting.

All Saints blesses animals inside the church during worship service for the Feast of St Francis in early October, and will even bless stuffed animals on request. Recently two braying beagles took first place in joining the baritone section of the choir. Most cats attend by sending their human "staff" with feline glamour shots. Trust All Saints here; it's better that way. A gray African parrot and a miniature horse remain two of the priest's favorite guests. The interior church has remained "accident free" despite decades of potential mishaps. This is considered a modern day miracle.

The church members continue the tradition of late night Christmas Eve services with that Currier and Ives Christmas nostalgia. Cold weather, the crunch of snow underfoot and the warmth of carols sustain homecomings year by year. On Palm Sunday you can watch All Saints take to the street waving palms and singing, "All Glory, Laud and Honor." This makes the corner of Washington and 5th even more dangerous for pedestrians and drivers gawking as bundled and coated parishioners pretend a spring-like Easter is just a week away!

A highlight of summer is the San Jose Obrero Mission for seasonal workers at the Montgomery packing plant, in its 23rd year; a church service and meal is served to eighty tired folks responsible for getting corn canned for grocery shelves. All Saints was known for its hospitality over the years. And known for decades for the best funeral lunches in town.

When we think of the QUAKERS, we think of LaNelle and Ken Olson and Eleanor Zelliot, the ones we first knew; also, AnnaLisa and Charles Tooker. And Mac (Alden) and Margaret McCutchan who hosted many

‖‖

POLICE LOG, July 12. The Northfield Fire department ventilated a building in the 1300 block of Bollenbacher Drive after somebody accidentally discharged pepper spray on the second floor.

Meeting events at their Sogn Valley farm. As Northfield prospered after the Civil War, many Northfield churches were built in or near Washington Street, around Third to Fifth Street, known at that time as Christian Hill. Cannon Valley Friends Meeting completed their own Meeting House on Washington Street in fall 2014. While being built, it had windows marked with red diamonds, saying Integrity, certainly a Quaker trait, but the diamonds turned out to be only ads for Integrity by Marvin Windows. The Friends Meeting House may help us restore the territory.

Like many Quaker meetings, Northfield Friends have no paid staff. Friends worship together in silence seeking an inner sense of Truth, some calling it God, Spirit, the divine, or the Light within. Sometimes worshipers share a message out of that silence. Worship motivates Friends to embody and work toward simplicity, peace, integrity, community, equality and stewardship. They celebrate their first permanent home in Northfield after more than a half-century meeting in homes and rented spaces.

When the First Congregational Church of Northfield caught fire in 1880 some townspeople thought the James Gang had returned, as promised, to revenge their defeat in Northfield. It was hot ashes on an old roof that really was to blame. The First Congregational Church on the corner of 3rd and Union was dedicated in December 1881.

From its formation in 1856 the congregation was committed to international mission projects. Programs for the Northfield area were also planned by church members and often housed within their buildings, such as the gymnasium—the first in town, in their 1908 addition. Other projects like the Clothes Closet, Senior Dining and Community Action were also begun at the church. Newcomers to Northfield were invited to what was called the Congo-Baptist Church, an informal arrangement that benefited both congregations and lasted until the church officially became the First United Church of Christ, Northfield. It's a real community, with a little garden in front offering food you might want (who's been eating those sunflowers?), and even turns its parking lot into a community stomping ground, with Food Trucks on Tuesdays, a place to retire ancient electronic devices on some Saturday afternoons, and flea markets sometimes on Jesse James Days.

The United Methodist Church has a long history in our area, beginning in a log cabin on the edge of the woods in 1855, soon moving to the Joseph Drake home and farm. In 1856, their first Northfield home was in a schoolhouse at 300 Union, where the UCC now stands. Beginning in 1918, joint Baptist, Methodist, and Congregationalist services were held there until 1919. The church has a remarkable tour of its various homes in Northfield on its website, and following it provides an interesting history of our town.

In 1859, the Methodists built their own church around the area of 316 East Sixth between College and Union. At that time it overlooked a pond, called "The Methodist Pond." The church that stood here was remembered in the *Northfield News* in 1897 as "…more like a small barn with windows on the side than a modern house of worship. The inside… was the plainest of plain; no electric lights, no carpets, no papered, painted or frescoed walls, no cushioned seats or upholstered furniture adorned the inside of this pioneer church, but into this modest, homely, and unpretentious building was put the labor of love and self-sacrifice of the men, women and children of the church, and they were proud of it and loved it with a love that few people feel for the church today." At that time, this was the only church building in Northfield, and the Methodists generously shared it with the Congregationalists and the Baptists.

The parsonage on East Sixth Street was destroyed by fire, and a new parsonage was built at Third and Washington in 1875. It later became the Skaar apartment house. In 1877 the old church on Sixth Street was sold, and construction was started on a new church adjacent to the parsonage. It was dedicated in 1883 to serve an expanding congregation.

In 1924, the old church from Third and Washington was moved to Third and Winona, remodeled and dedicated in September. A former residence of Carleton President F. B. Hill had been purchased and turned into Parish House, with offices and education wing of the church. By 1946, part of the Parish House was used as an apartment for the pastor's family; the old parsonage on Washington Street was sold. In 1951 a new parsonage was built, just to the west of the Parish House. The current church building and parsonage were constructed about 1965 on farmland at the edge of Northfield, which can now be seen at 1401 and 1411 Maple. The architect was Edward Sovik, a Northfield architect who gained international recognition for similar church plans and the Methodists have the only Sovik church in town. The Methodists are known for two handbell choirs, one for youth, and for Super Wednesdays, with a Kid's Club, a Middle School and a High School fellowship, a shared dinner, and a knitting group. There is now Weekly Silent Meditation Practice around the baptismal font on Thursdays.

Frank Wolf would be pleased to know that a student he taught statistics to at Carleton, the Rev. Kristin Maier, now serves as minister of the congregation he helped start. About fifty years ago, Professor Wolf and eleven other free thinkers formed the fledgling UNITARIAN UNIVERSALIST FELLOWSHIP OF NORTHFIELD. They welcomed people of any theological persuasion as they first met in each other's homes. Slowly but surely, the group grew and they moved to the Northfield Arts Guild, which eventually became a tight a squeeze once again.

Today, the UUs fill the Mason's hall every Sunday under the banner "Standing on the Side of Love." Theists, agnostics, atheists, and even Carls and Oles all come together to sing hymns and light candles of joy or concern. They reflect on what it means to care for the world and one's spirit, and they teach their children to respect all people and all religions. They have more than quintupled that original dozen. We'll have to see where they take their message of love next. It seems to be spreading; that sweet little house across the street from the UU's with all the flowers in the spring has a wire heart in the yard that says "I Love You."

Jewish children have had educational programming from time to time in Northfield. A few years ago, Alan Rubenstein formed the NORTHFIELD BEIT MIDRASH, the House of Study, and ran several reading groups over several years. Professor Laurence Cooper later joined Rubenstein to teach a Great Books winter term course at Carleton focusing on the Hebrew Bible. And at one time there was a half-hour prayer service once a week. The happy news is that if interest increases there is still a Northfield Beit Midrash which will remain to welcome interested students with Jewish education and services and all of the town.

There is a relatively new church, called the CANVAS CHURCH. Curious about the name? The Bible says that God had a plan for our lives, and that when we meet Jesus and His grace that we are promised a blank

POLICE LOG, *August 20. A Suspicious Activity: a caller in the 2700 block of Oak Lawn Drive said the same vehicle had driven by the house four times. An officer checked and found that it was a person teaching somebody to drive.*

canvas, a fresh start, with hope for the future and forgiveness for the past. "God is in the business of Re-building, Re-painting, Re-storing, and Re-deeming. We're in the business of God's business, so Northfield then became our corner of the world." The Canvas Church then became our latest pioneer.

REJOICE! was birthed by Hosanna Lutheran Church in Lakeville, in 2003. Rejoice! members (the exclamation point is mandatory) believe that we are all created for community, and that spiritual growth best happens in a small group of believers. There are small groups throughout the week, and prayer stations at every worship service, inviting anyone to come and be prayed for. Upbeat and spirited music is followed by a practical, biblically-based message. Another interesting feature of Rejoice! is what is called The Overflow, a time of extended worship through music, when the congregation is invited *to be more expressive*, to sing and pray *in the Spirit*, to be still in awed reverence, and authentically celebrate what is the overflow of their heart's response to God.

Many Northfield churches seemed to be changing their name. What if we walked in and everything was different?

Even EMMAUS BAPTIST CHURCH changed its name to Emmaus, welcoming a visit, and asked us to discover that this was a unique congregation full of surprises. The name Emmaus is taken from the New Testament story of two discouraged, grieving people who found hope in meeting a resurrected Jesus as they walked along the road together. No one will forget Emmaus because as we drive by there are three crosses on the small hill before we see the church.

Pastor Amy, who left several years ago, sparked up the MORAVIAN CHURCH by adding the words Main Street, a welcoming message that you didn't need to be Moravian to go there. The topics she courageously covered for teenagers and others made Moravians Modern. You might be interested to learn that Moravia is a historical country in Central Europe in the east of the Czech Republic and one of the historical Czech lands, together with Bohemia and Czech Silesia. This represents yet another European group that came to Northfield. The church truly comes alive during the Christmas season. On the first Thursday in December, during Northfield's Winter Walk, church members stand in snow and cold proclaiming that the Christ Child has been born! Everyone can come, dress up and share in an enactment of the birth of Jesus, with costumes, scenery, lights, narration, a "slightly insane leadership," and a Chili Feed. Also during this season the church returns to its history with a traditional Moravian service of story and song, following the old custom of singing the Moravian Hymn "Morning Star," led by a child and sung responsively with the congregation. The other tradition observed at this time is the candle light service, with beeswax candles lit during the singing of "Joy to the World," and the lights dimmed while everyone sings "Morning Star" and "Silent Night."

The Church also takes its turn in a worldwide Moravian prayer tradition called the Unity Prayer Watch, organized so that at every hour of every day throughout the year, somewhere in the world there is at least one Moravian in prayer for the needs of the world and the church.

THE CORNERSTONE ALLIANCE CHURCH was nearby, with an open arms congregation, even if you weren't a Christian. Just as the Moravian Church, it had modernized with a new name.

And then there was LIFE21 on Jefferson Road. Once again, a mystifying name change, maybe more than once. Not too long ago it was the Gospel of Life Family Church. If you're driving along Jefferson Road, if you're still trying to figure it out, Think. And it becomes a great surprise. Definitely modernizing. Life21 has a very good history of wonderful congregations that have had a real impact on the city of Northfield. They now have gone through a transition and are redeveloping a vision and rebuilding into a revival-type church. Their new vision includes mentoring courses to help one become a good citizen and then reach out to others in need. They've also opened their doors to a Spanish Church that uses the facility when the congregation is not using the building.

CITY LIGHT CHURCH, called New Covenant Church until 2008, hosts a family-oriented congregation with contemporary worship and a charismatic atmosphere. It's enjoyable to look at photos of the congregation and see so many significant Northfielders who had been in the church since its birth. City Light, although once a new church, boasts many long-time members. The current pastor is Peter Haase. It has been enjoyable getting to know the church by reading a blog about some of the church's activities in its past. The City Light Church had been blessed with new ideas for church services, especially in the summer, enough to make everyone join in the "fun," without forgetting they were still in church. Remembering the progressive dinners of yore, the

church members once had a Progressive Church, the Church on the Bus.
After two songs and announcements, they loaded a rented bus and traveled to Bridge Square, City Hall, and other places, with short services at
every location. The younger children really enjoyed their first trip on a
school bus. Another great idea was Super-Hero Sunday, where after the
morning service, there were tables where everyone could sit, invent, and
draw a favorite Super-Hero. There was Joshua, Rehab, and Noah, and a
flipbook and a comic book in the shape of a cross.

Lutherans remained strong, not changing their names, even after
Thrivent Financial changed theirs.

If ever there was a Lutheran Cathedral it would be SAINT JOHN's. It
began as Saint Johannes, which is even more romantic. Its early choir,
filled with the ranks of St. Olaf students and faculty, inspired F. Melius Christiansen, who soon reorganized it into the St. Olaf Lutheran
Choir, which now fills the world with music, even with the Lutheran
part missing. Norwegians found their voice. St. John's carries the spirit
of great Norwegian-Americans, such as Edward Sovik, the Northfield
architect who left some parts of his great architectural work with America's churches in his home church. Saint John's was the Westminster
Abbey of Norwegian-Americans. (Remembering Edward Sovik, whose
spirit remains in this church, brings back a memory of seeing him, long
after retirement, seated in a restaurant with Northfield's younger architects. It was as if we were watching a Master. St. John's, the churches he
built, and the architects who continued to learn from him are his legacy.

And St. John's can be lotsafun, especially in summer when Guy Reid
announces the High and Holy days for a fruit festival. She starts a month
before Rhubarb Sunday to make her announcement. And Strawberry
Sunday, is the most exciting when she wears a red dress sprinkled with
little black flecks like a big strawberry. Before Apple Sunday, asking for
volunteers, she wears an apple green top.

BETHEL was the music and singing church. The violins and strings
are amazing, the Bell Choir continues to grow. There are choirs for all
ages, and on the grounds you will see a sculpture by Mac Gimse. Bethel's

POLICE LOG, *August 29. Shoplifting reported at Econofoods after a 19-year old
man took a magazine into the bathroom and left it there.*

pastor ends each sermon by saying "God loves you and so do I." As part of Bethel folklore, the choir director can playfully alter this message for the joy of it.

There was TRINITY LUTHERAN, Missouri Synod. We were charmed by its Little Lambs preschool, with its emphasis on Bible stories, a sweet place for children to grow, and with open arms, inviting the whole community to their Easter Egg hunt. At Christmas the little lambs dressed like very authentic shepherds, others dressed like lambs, and there was an angel and Joseph and Mary and baby Jesus.

ST. PETER's was founded by Danish immigrants in 1893, first meeting in their homes and later in the church on West 3rd street that is now the Northfield Arts Guild Theatre. Since they are now more diverse, it might be fun to count their Danes. They're known for the Heavenly Hoedown in September when everyone gets their Cowboy on.

ST. DOMINIC's CATHOLIC CHURCH became the joyous church, especially after it welcomed yet a new community, with loads of precious children. You can be invited to experience that joy, especially when you're invited to the celebration of Our Lady of Guadalupe, or La Posada with a real baby. Father Denny had the passion and the language to serve our new Spanish-speaking community, starting by visiting the newcomers in their homes, the apartments on the edge of town, and then from trailer to trailer in Viking Terrace and Florella's.

Later came the Spanish mass. The new people began making lists of their favorite songs, and organizing the music themselves. The accompaniment went from piano to guitar, bass, tambourine and drums. St. Dominic now has four lively musical groups who play at home and at other parishes.

The largest part of the Spanish-speaking community turned out to be from the same town and parish in Mexico: San Pedro Apóstol in Maltrata, Veracruz, as well as in other towns and cities within 25 miles away. Father Denny in his second year began making an annual visit to Maltrata, staying in the homes of the families of our Northfield residents.

St. Dominic's became a safe place for its new population to celebrate life and faith, a little more like the Catholic churches of 40 or 50 years ago where those who worship became a beautiful circle of friends, so hanging around the church is pretty common. People aren't in a big rush to get on to something else. And for Father Denny, they are like family as well, which he says is part of his reward for investing his life in theirs.

And if you love hearing church music, the NTV coverage of the St. Dominic's Spanish Mass will bring you joy—Sunday nights at 10PM.

Reverend Arthur Hill from the UNITED METHODIST CHURCH at Stanton gave us not only a science lesson but a delicious absence of dogma, allowing us to blame the dirty snow (those dark colored particulates, dust, dirt and sand) as drifts from the sky rather than on snow plowing or automobiles. These particles were always there, but showed up when it got warm. Who knew? Reverend Hill wrote in the *Northfield News* that there had to be an Easter-like parable in this, and hoped we could find it. It'a fun to honor an open-thinker like that.

And Northfield has a swami! Gracia Gimse began yoga in Thailand when she was fourteen and discovered meditation in a Zen monastery in Japan in the fifth grade. Yoga was not simply a physical thing for Gracia since it began with meditation and as the years went by it became truly spiritual. After years of teaching yoga, she went to Seminary at the Temple of Kriya Yoga, where they teach philosophy combined with physical practice. A swami helps others find their way in connecting with the spirit, creates rituals at significant times in life, such as welcoming a baby into the world or making a new life transition.

Many things remain sacred in our town: the Margaret Evans Huntington Club, Valley Grove, the Farmer's Market. We have Saints to Preserve: Father Denny, Maggie Lee, Will Healy, Dixon Bond, F. Mellius Christianssen who founded the St. Olaf Choir, John North, and Toff (a cat saint), Abbie and Steve Meierbachtol, the math saints who year after year gave tirelessly of their time and energy to inspire new generations with their passion for mathematics. Toff was the only one with a statue and a postcard and John North had his own publicist: Arthur Paul David White. And there was Dan Freeman, also known as Mr. Northfield. He was the only saint who had a life-size cut-out that was provided by the Freeman Fireworks Endowment Fund, so that Northfielders could take their picture with him on Townie Night just before Jesse James Days.

Maggie Lee had a poem written about her: "A Candle for Maggie Lee." The second stanza reads:

All these extravagant iolite existences now carry
the tinge of you, Maggie Lee; hold your memory
in their shadows: your life
touches mine as I walk beside the flowing Cannon River
or pause on stairs imagined by you, here in my town,
your town, our town, where there is, it seems, a constant well
of beauty, purpling and ethereal, renewed and renewing as
the hot petunias in the civic baskets will,
do, as drifts of phlox in the Carleton Arb
and that sunset band of cloud on the St. Olaf hill.

Leslie Schultz

Maggie Lee's relics were spread throughout Northfield after her cat memorabilia auction—all 5,000 of them, with proceeds donated to the Northfield Historical Society and the Prairie's Edge Humane Society.

Okay, they were just Northfield saints, but they might be accepted by all denominations, and we didn't pray to them.

We often feared that the Margaret Evans Huntington Club (sometimes known as MEH (Not hot, Not not, Just Meh) might publish its own "meh list" aiming at stuff we once loved, or words we used:

1. sammich
2. significant other
3. veggies
4. the word amazing

We always wanted a first peek at the club's book choices for reading the next year. In Northfield, "What are you reading?" was as close as we got to the Red Carpet's "Who are you wearing?"

<hr>

POLICE LOG, August 30. Missing or lost mail reported in the 700 block of North Highway 3. As it turns out, the mailman had not been there.

NORTHFIELD RITUALS

J UST AS THE CHURCHES HAD RITUALS, NORTHFIELD HAD THEM TOO, its quirky or whimsical ways of doing things, and somehow the Defeat of Jesse James Days continued to bring it the most attention. You probably would not have come here without somehow hearing the story. The re-enactment of the defeat was the most important part, and may we say right here we hope that there will always be three generations of DeManns riding in it. It was so much a part of Northfield identity that a re-enactment can be tacked on at other times to other events, including the Taste of Northfield spring celebration. Maintaining the historical accuracy of these re-enactments was a matter of religion and woe be it to he who wears an inauthentic cowboy hat or the wrong duster. Some years ago an attempt to involve the ladies by inviting them to dress up as saloon girls got a few folks in trouble. In 1876 there were no such establishments and no such ladies in Northfield. However, now there are many mothers and children in nineteenth century clothes walking the streets as part of the background of the drama. Many Minnesota towns had their own celebrations, but this was better than the

Hopkins Raspberry Festival; at least one time when eager tourists went there the only raspberry in town was a raspberry shake at Dairy Queen.

After hearing all the variations of the Jesse James story, we also enjoyed the extra bits that had been left out; Willam Pye's description of the men who participated in stopping the raid was extremely moving. As a boy Pye knew most of the men who participated. "Each one of them was, in a way, a character and I believe that Northfield at that time contained more men of outstanding types than any town of its size in Minnesota. They were full of humor, had strong convictions, had a thorough knowledge of national affairs and were typical pioneers, and the sons of pioneers."

> Jay Huyck: I'm so Northfield I send out dead on the slab postcards of the James gang as Christmas cards.
>
> Chris: I'm so Northfield, I've seen Cole Younger's EAR.
>
> John Fossum; I'm so Northfield I know it's not Cole Younger's ear.
>
> Chris: I'm so Northfield that I STILL BELIEVE it was Cole Younger's ear.
>
> John Fossum: Charlie Pitts was also not the skeleton in Schilling Museum which is now at the Northfield Historical Society:
>
> Chris: I'm so Northfield, John Fossum can HAVE my skeleton.

We especially enjoyed what Pye later told about some of the stories he had heard about the robbery that he had left out. About a man who threw stones at the robbers; about the man who had no firearms but shook his fist at them and swore; about the man who came right out on the square with an old rusty gun and shot it at them, and was so drunk that the robbers paid no attention to him. Sometimes we wish the re-enactment would bring these guys back. There were numerous stories of this sort from W.W. Pye, the local attorney, from a 1947 talk he gave to the Rice County Historical Society.

Kai Carlson-Wee grew up in Northfield, later rollerbladed professionally, surfed north of the Arctic Circle, traveled across the country by freight train, and ended up teaching poetry at Stanford. His poem, *Jesse James Days*, a love song to his brother, was a prizewinner. As kids, that celebration was an opportunity to run around with cap guns, act like outlaws and pretend their Huffys were horses, and although his poem is much longer, here he describes the re-enactment:

> And watching the staged reenactment at sunset, the over-
> groomed horse and amplified pleadings of Heywood refusing
> to open the safe. Refusing to hear what it meant
> they would do to him — carving an X in his collarbone,
> cracking his skull with the butt of a gun.
> The teller lying dead in a puddle of blood
> beside him. The sound of the bullet that ripped off his ear,
> more a physical weight than a sound, a texture of things
> growing suddenly far away, fattening, filled with a needling buzz.
> The ease with which he could picture those three
> silent numbers, floating like neon-lit billboards against
> the darkening lids of his eyes. Really just simple
> abstractions, marks on a chalkboard, lines in a ledger that
> nobody else,
> besides himself and the wealthy proprietor
> who sometimes stopped in on Sundays
> with his twin boys to look at the weekly reports,
> could read. Do you remember the way the horses were trained
> to carefully lower their heads, to give us the softest part of
> their jaws,
> regardless of whether we carefully touched them
> or offered them handfuls of grain?

Early on Saturdays, even before the re-enactment, there was the Children's Parade, with the children dressed in costume. Certainly the sweetest part of all the festivities. One old favorite was when Jack Thurn-blad dressed his grandchildren and had them play little games of basket-ball as they ran along. The Defeat of Jesse James Day parade on Sunday was also a great part of the festival. Another special feature of the past had been the St. Paul Vulcan Krewe, some on motorcycles. Our memo-ries of them might be wrong, but it seemed that they'd kiss women and

---

POLICE LOG, September 2. Somebody poured ranch dressing on a vehicle at Cub Foods, 2423 Hwy 3.

leave black marks on their faces, and at that innocent time it was fun to go home with one of those marks, when we were seriously uninformed about woman as object. Here's hoping those funlovin' boys didn't get charged with sexual harassment, but they don't come around anymore.

THE NORTHFIELD CALENDAR

You'll love to start the school year with the Defeat of Jesse James Days. Right after that, when the swimming pool closes for people, there is the Doggy Swim, guaranteeing each dog of all size, shape and age a good time. Later there are the Lutefisk lunches and dinners at Vang Lutheran Church. Driving and first seeing that church close to sunset feels like a pilgrimage to Chartres. There is the Crop Walk in October, to raise funds to relieve hunger. There might be a St. Olaf homecoming parade on Division Street where we always hope the President would lead the parade with those big flags, but he was usually in the car with his wife throwing out beads like they do in New Orleans. Later you can go to Cemetery Stories at Halloween, on to the community Thanksgiving dinner. You can celebrate St. Lucia's Day—enjoy the Winter Walk by candlelight and the St. Olaf Christmas Festival, its music later to be shared with the world. This is combined with a Scandinavian feast where you can see hundreds of Norwegian sweaters on both men and women (and perhaps one or two glamorous women in black and stilettos, who hadn't got the pitch) and then eat enough gravlax to last you for a year. If you must, you can relax for a while after that, go back to scrapbooking or have time alone on your ice floe, unless you join the sport of competitive snow shoveling. There's the Girl Scout Cookie Contests in Northfield offices in February—no more door to door with those cute little girls in uniform, just their moms and dads. And when it gets warmer, there's always the raffle based on betting who would be the last woman to discard her winter turtleneck. In March, if we're lucky there might be a St. Patrick's Day parade, which would be Jim McDonnell and some kids with green stuff on their trikes; perhaps if you have the luck of the Irish, it might end with Jim reading from Yeats at the Grand. It was said that St. Dominic in its beginning was half German and half Irish, but where are the Irish now? Or maybe we could create a tax inversion, and pretend we're Irish just like Medtronic did. Well, at least we now have Laura McKenzie who presents a Traditional Irish Music session weekly on Wednesdays in Grundy's Rueb'n'Stein with players and listeners welcome. However, our neighbor Kilkenny is the lucky place to be Irish. The thirty-two year old Mayor of Kilkenny, Ireland, Andrew McGuinness, came to Kilkenny, Minnesota for Half-Way to St. Paddy's Day wearing his Mayor's Chain, with each link representing a new mayor. The two Kilkennys officially became "Twin" cities in 2012.

In May, the height of the spring season was *syttende mai* at St. Olaf. The day celebrates the Norwegian constitution, signed on May 17, 1814, which started Norway's journey to becoming an independent nation following four hundred years as a Danish colony. The most moving part of the celebration, in addition to the Scandinavian food, is the singing of "Norge I rodt, hfitt og blatt," "Norway in Red, White and Blue." The song was sung subversively during the Second World War when Norwegians were not allowed to sing their national anthem. Esther Hustvedt was once jailed in Norway for singing that song, and on more than one occasion spoke about it after she came to Northfield. The courageous song tells that although Norway cannot show its colors, the red, white and blue in nature keeps their spirits high. The women who come to the May 17th celebration wear their bunads, complete with jewelry, Andrea Een plays the hardanger fiddle and it's a warming experience (although not part of the program) to watch Dagfinn Moe walk around the tables loving to talk in Norwegian, especially to the male Norwegian international students, there in their black suits. For several hours we're in Norwegian himmel, strangers that we are. For Dagfinn's latest big birthday party, his Norwegian family here for the special celebration was shocked and amazed when the Northfield guests, one and almost all, broke out into the Norwegian national anthem. Someone said it was like the scene in Casablanca. Julie Thorsheim said maybe everyone learned it at the Sons of Norway.

In early summer comes the Taste of Northfield, the Fourth of July celebration, Paul Niemisto's gift to Northfield, the Vintage Band Festival (12 bands in 12 hours in one special year) and then there's Crazy Days. Some Minnesota communities, in reaction to Midnight Madness and Crazy Days that were driving them nuts decided to celebrate Sane Days instead. When you go through Minnesota towns, if a Sane Day is in progress the signs will be unmistakable. Very few people will be on the streets. The stores will be dimly lit. When you enter, the store's owner will say: "Are you going to buy anything?" If you say yes, the merchant will turn on the rest of the lights. Nothing will be on sale. Late in August there are noon organ recitals in the churches.

HISTORIC NORTHFIELD WEDDINGS, PARTIES, AND FUNERALS

And don't forget Northfielders' weddings, with each one having a distinguishing feature. There was Eric's and Claire's, a tribute to Dr. Seuss, by honest Eric, who, although he had written a whole book on Larry Gould, took no credit for writing this:

Will you answer us right now
These questions, as your wedding vow?

E & C (together): Yes, we will answer now
Your questions as our wedding vow.

Will you take Eric as your spouse?
Will you share with him your house?

Yes, I take him as my spouse.
Sharing life within our house.

Will you take Claire as your wife?
Will you love her all your life?

Yes, I take her as my wife,
Yes, I'll love her all my life....

Will you love through good and bad?
Whether you're happy or whether you're sad?

Yes, I'll love through good and bad,
Whether we're happy or whether sad...

Will you love him if you're rich?
Or if you're poor, and in a ditch?

Yes, I'll love him if we're rich,
And I will love him in a ditch,
I'll love him through good times and bad,
Whether we are happy or sad...

And I will love her when we're rich
And I will love her in a ditch
And I will love through good and bad,
And I will love when glad or sad...
Yes, I will love for my whole life
This lovely woman as my wife!...

And I will love him when we're rich,
And when we're broke and in a ditch...

Then if you'll take *her* as your wife,
And if you'll love her all your life,
And you'll take *him* to be your hubby,
Whether he's thin or grows kind of tubby...
And if you'll love through good and bad,
And whether you're happy or whether sad,
And love in sickness, and in health,
And when you're poor, and when in wealth,
And if you'll love with all your heart,
From now until death do you part,
Yes, if you'll both love through and through,
Please answer with the words "I DO."

I DO!

I DO TOO!

If you wanted a bilingual wedding, Father Denny of St. Dominic's can make a pleasant transition in the ceremony from English to Spanish.

When Tania and Mike got married, bride, groom, and guests led by a violinist paraded from St. John's, across the bridge to Division Street to the Northfield Armory. The place was decorated like a high school prom, and the tables were decorated with copies of old wedding photos, a Japanese custom, with a nod to ancestors. It was great fun to guess who all the ancestors were.

When Andrea and Ron were married, after the ceremony they went down the aisles shaking hands with all the guests who had come.

Qiguang and Litao celebrated their marriage in Northfield and were carried together from the chapel in a rickshaw, following their poetic vows:

Qiguang:

No matter how great or humble people may be, when their life ends, their tombstones have only two dates; their birthday and the day of death. Before and after the two dates is the endless and unknown world. Between them is a short and straight dash, a dash representing the whole life, concealing hopes and disappointments, covering accomplishments and failures, burying shames and glories. But now I see that fate has granted me the third date. Today, will be carved in the middle of the dash of my life. It marks the beginning of a flower-studded path under a starry sky. On this date of departure and at the beginning of this long journey to the limit of the possible, I vow to my traveling companion of life and dear wife:

Litao:

I will love you and reach the end of life's journey with you.

I will respect you and share with you every minute of happiness and sadness, challenge and success.

I will love you and make contributions to the world with you.

I will respect you and grow together with you in obtaining knowledge, thought, health, and experiences.

Qiguang:

We were not born on the same day, and probably would not leave the world on the same day either. But in between them we share a date more important and splendid. This is today when our souls have touched, combined, and sublimated. May the people under heaven who love each other have what we have: a date that makes their hearts soar like an eagle, a date higher than life and death.

One of Northfield's best home-made weddings was Gigi and Geoff's at Valley Grove. Gigi found a wedding dress from the Carleton theater, both mothers made chicken curry, and the wedding took place in both churches—vows in one, dinner in the other. The floor in the second church was tilted, which caused the layers of the wedding cake to start sliding. The family had to bring in everything, not just the food, but all chairs, tables, silverware, glasses, water, plates and cups. There was no running water, and only an outhouse for facilities. They borrowed dishes from the college, brought them all home and spread them out on the lawn, rinsed them off with a hose, after which all their neighbors washed them in their home dishwashers. Susan Bauer led a Maypole dance, and Michel Monnot, who had begun the wedding in a wheelchair, was one of the dancers. Jackson said it was just like a little English village. There was a classical music quartet in the graveyard, and as the children started playing there, it began to look like an Ingmar Bergmann movie.

When Paul and Melissa got married in St. Olaf's Urness Hall, Paul gave a dramatic reading from Shakespeare during the ceremony, but at the reception, Melissa surprised him by singing "Do I Hear a Waltz" from a 1965 musical of the same name. Paul was greatly surprised, and for everyone there, they'll probably remember it forever.

And of course there were parties, but you had to keep those invitations secret because maybe your friends weren't going. Some were not forgotten. That party where the St. Olaf male German professor waltzed with a Carleton male Religion professor. There was the birthday party where Karen Wee gave her good friend a wooden bowl of wooden cherries, a tribute to what Life Is or Can Be on good days. These parties usually climaxed with women breaking into dance.

And there was Lydia's birthday, where the ever-delightful Ross Shoger began to sing: "Oooooooh, Lydia oh Lydia, say, have you met Lydia, Lydia, the Tattooed Lady. She has eyes that folks adore so, And a torso even more so. Lydia oh Lydia, that encyclopedia, Oh Lydia the Queen of Tattoo." And little did Ross know what a sentimental tribute that was since Lydia had heard that song ever since she was a toddler, sitting on her uncle's lap.

If you wanted something special at your party you could ask our friend Jo to stand on her head and sing Happy Birthday.

MINNEAPOLIS STAR TRIBUNE, September 26. Northfield: A caller in the 1800 block of Truman Court reported that a neighbor's cat keeps coming over... Police agreed to contact the owner...

There was party where a fun feminist brand of invitation said that men should come dressed as animals just as a joke and some of them did. However, most of our parties were just fantasy parties. We'd make an exciting list of people we'd love to invite and then find many reasons for not doing it, including having to clean the house. One hostess's husband was well-known, however, for cleaning the house by vacuuming before anyone left. This reminded us of the Fabulous Lynda at the Byzantine, when we'd say "Oh, we'll just sit here and talk until two, at which point she would say, "No, you don't." Lynda was also famous for never giving out a recipe. However, it was always fun to close a restaurant at night with a good friend. It was also fun to spy on parties, check out the guests and decide how they got there: League of Women Voters? Came to Northfield the same year? Have children the same age? Margaret Evans friends? Same field as the guest speaker? Pay back?

Even our funerals had that little special twist. Jim Koehler's service ended in a pizza lunch, and gave old Northfield students a chance to write about what a great teacher Jim was, and for all of us to learn and perhaps celebrate for the first time the golden days of the NHS English department. Fresh from King Tut, two loving and fun sisters filled their mother's grave with Reese's Pieces and handfuls of pistachios. Another buried her mom in a nightgown because that was her favorite thing to wear. Dixon Bond's service had songs from the Carleton Knights, all from many different years, presided over by invited guests Dan Dressen (a St. Olaf pretend Knight in a tuxedo) and Dan Kallman as well as Judy Bond's early singing group gathering together after many years. Dixon's sister appeared with a huge binder, threatening the mourners with a long eulogy, but it was all in fun. Dixon also had brought the Knights and helped to orchestrate Dacie Moses's service; somehow this might have been the first to be called a celebration of life, since Dacie had lived for a wonderful long time. Paul Fjelstad's Quaker service was complete with hilarious stories of this great man's eccentricities, and at the lunch which followed, when his son Kaj was asked if he still juggled, Kaj quickly picked up six clementines and proved that he did.

Even retirement parties had special touches. Anne Ulmer had her tai chi group all in their great new t-shirts come, show what they could do, and join her celebration.

NORTHFIELD'S POPULATION

NORTHFIELD WAS CRAWLING WITH RETIRED PEOPLE, SOME OF whom were also poets — at least on our sidewalk. Now they're overwintering, just like robins. Northfield Life was so darn good that even snowbirds wouldn't miss out on too much. Let them eat snow! We honored our Greatest Generation with heroes like Bill Cupp, Jack Thurnblad, Harvey Elling. Our Northfield Greatest Generation organized the Last Man's Club: Bernie Wierson, Chuck DeMann, John Moe, Erling Kindem, Howard Sargent, Art Haugen, Doug Pflaum, and Alan Kump. We had Vietnam vets, a VFW, and still had a nice group of the Great Generation of Army clerk typists. Another hero, Ross Stickley, went back to the 65th anniversary of his service at the Berlin Blockade.

They deserve front seats everywhere they go and to insure that, retired citizens always came at least forty minutes early. They were wonderful volunteers. When you'd thank them for all they were doing, they'd simply answer with our favorite Charlie Black joke: "Ah shucks, what's time to a pig?" Still they had been warned not to wear pink since fashion experts cautioned that if you have any hint of pink in your face, wearing pink makes you look like a piglet. (*New York Times*, July 27, 2014) Even these experienced volunteers probably didn't know that if you hurt a pig's feelings it takes two weeks for the pig to get over it, and who knew about them? But did they know something we didn't? It turns out that helping out brings true happiness. Spending money on yourself "barely moves the needle," but spending time or money on others hits the target. Giving improves the belief that you can handle a situation, solve problems, not just be a bystander or a victim of circumstance. That's what research says.

Years ago, there weren't any retired people around, and there's certainly no American Association of non-Retired Persons for the rest of you. However, if you're now over fifty and have a card, don't let it be seen when you open your wallet on your Match.com date. Remember, too, AARP's now chasing after the boomers. And if you join you'll get their magazine and their newsletter and you're going to have to read too many stories too many times about how great it is to be old. AARP now has its own comfy dating service. Our retired people once left town to protect themselves, not wanting to share the humiliation, looking from the outside in, trying to get to know those people who are inside looking out, escaping to new places filled with other old people. Now Northfield has a fabulous cohort, threatening a takeover. Retired people formed clubs in self-defense. They were the majority in Sons of Norway and knew its national anthem. They had emeriti professor clubs, and the indefatigable Alice Thomas (that someone so indefatigable thinks that we all are indefatigable, too) formed a Tuesday club for the emeriti spouses, usually called the Trophy Wives for short. UCC had a men's book club. So much was always going on. The CVEC sounds like yet another medical appliance so famous in Minnesota, but it's Northfield's own educational organization with many classes, best called the Elder Collegium. Hungry people came from as far away as Faribault and Lakeville to make up for what they were missing. It's where retired professors could finally take courses from their former colleagues and discover, perhaps for the first time, what good teachers they were. They could teach loads of subjects. Ed Sostek had a great theater course called "Lets Go to the Theater and Try to Remember What we Saw." Hartley Clark, who became a specialist in the Arab Spring, finally told the Arabs: "You're on your own," and switched to lecturing on the wonders of Italy. But then

POLICE LOG, October 17. Writing found in Bible referring to a missing person in Canada reported in the 1000 block of Cedar Avenue.

we hear he's coming back again. The Spring was over, but the world was worse.

CHILDREN, OUR FUTURE UNTIL THEY LEAVE

The best part of Northfield is the children, the hope for our future between the time they graduated and before they left town. Their infancy was doula-free, although the hyper-moms recorded their Apgar scores. They thrived on pomegranate and quinoa. We cherished them as they began their lives, and until they were old enough to leave home. They had a good start in their Daddy and Me classes, and adventurous daddies entered them in the annual Temper Tantrum contests and there were many white ribbons. As babies, their brains were built by black and white objects. They could see from birth, but it was high contrast colors, black and white that encouraged their visual development, as well as physical activities such as kicking and arm waving. When Lucy's husband Arch heard this, he pulled out his old Periodical Table of Elements for their twins, Ann and Easton.

When our children began to talk, they started most sentences with "Actually." There were some children who worried their parents because they didn't talk until later, and when they did, it was a comforting surprise. This was especially true with twins. When asked why they had waited, one said: "Everything was all right until now," and his silent brother said: "You're not the only pebble on the beach." It's true, our children could learn a lot of new words if they went to the right upscale daycare, where naptime was called "rejuvenation." Lunch was "Replenishment." "Free expression" was another word for tearing around the building. When they got bored with our baby talk, they'd beg for time-outs. Northfield streets lit up when the daycare children went on little walks around the town.

Many children demanded tvg (textured vegetable protein) in the school cafeteria. They wouldn't do a darn thing unless you said "Good Job." We kept them hooked on phonics. Although we voted to improve their education, they assured us that after fourth grade, all they needed was Wikipedia. After reading some writings of third graders, it seemed to be even earlier. Hannah Farmer, who as a third grader wrote:

MY CARE

My parents are who I care about. No person can replace them,
not even a mouse. I would be mournful inside, lonely and hun-
gry. Family dinners are cheerful times. I would miss all that, yes
I would. Without my parents my heart would be a black socket.
My lungs would be like Jell-O sinking with a frown. That's why
I care, oh yes I do. Hannah Farmer.

In addition, that wonderful book of Northfield History that you can
get at the Northfield Historical Society was written by middle schoolers
for third graders, and Northfield adults found it just perfect for them. By
the third grade, the children could have their own cellphones and send
back sweet little elfies of themselves on the playground. Some of these
children were so smart that very early they became our bosses, not our
employees.

But even Northfield's young were kind and generous. The Young
Buddhists adopted part of Highway 19, and after they left for college,
Northfield Montessori took over. We worried about those little tykes
cleaning up right after the speed limit changed to 45 mph, and after
a long while it was re-adopted. But thank you, Young Buddhists, and
Montessori. Now it's Cory Vititoe and Friends.

DNA APPLES NOT FAR FROM THE TREE

Genetics did not immediately make a difference. *The New York Times*,
writing about a study of surnames, found out that social mobility was
very slow. There no longer seems to be a working class. If you listen to
politicians, all we've got left is the middle class and those people who
own their own planes. However, we still cared about equality, as they
did somewhere in California where they banned Peter Rabbit because
Peter was too much an upper-class bunny. But according to the book
The Son Also Rises, social mobility can be predicted not only because of
your parental status, but also from your great great grandparents. Family
names tell you a lot. A study of surnames based on people of high pro-
fessional status revealed that Northfield had none of the top three global surnames—Shetty, Agarwal, and Gupta. And of the Selected High
Status Global Surnames, we had no Girgis, Cherlans, Khourys, Rahimi,
or Dizons. We didn't even have a Katz or a Kim. We had one Wang, one

Owusu, but no Papadopoulos. Maybe if any Katzes or Kims come to Tyvek Town, we could pull out the old Welcome Wagon again and give them some coupons.

Genetics seemed to pop out in unexpected places, or is it just falling not far from the tree? Alex Robins wore a suit and tie to his first three weeks of high school. His grandfather wore a suit and tie during his first few months at Carleton and announced that he was secretly married, and that his wife lived in Evans. But apparently this didn't hurt Alex, who was interviewed a few years after in a "Conversation with Alex Robins, Boy Wonder." He described turning *Waiting for Godot* into *Waiting for Charlie* into a five minute sketch in English class, with one kid pulling off his shirt and throwing it at the audience and two others jumping around the stage pounding each other while Alex remained in the center trying to hold an existentialist soirée. The fearless Alex reported that the punishment for inciting riot at the middle school was not being allowed to play dodgeball that day. When Alex was asked if he were going to college, he replied that college was for nerds. He wanted to go do a Jack Kerouac abroad: "On the Autobahn" or something.

SCANDINAVIANS IN NORTHFIELD

Having a Scandinavian-sounding name in Northfield might serve you well. At your choice of any Lutheran Church, it might immediately help you make some productive friendships. Much to our surprise, it wasn't always that way in Northfield. There apparently was a time when Scandinavimania had not taken hold. Northfielders hadn't always secretly wished they were Scandinavian and named their sons Eric or Soren or Anders. Jack Bunday, who played with Maggie Lee in their childhood days, told about the day Maggie once wandered across the street into Mrs. Nystuen's kitchen, when she was making lefse. She offered Maggie one with powdered sugar. Maggie declined. She was afraid that if she ate it she would turn into a Norwegian. But Jack reported that "By the time I left Northfield for Chicago I realized that prejudice against Nor-

CARLETON SECURITY BLOTTER, October 14. At 10:15 pm, Security received a phone call from a student reporting that the student's roommate had been involved in a "huge fight on the Internet" and needed medical attention.

wegians was absurd." Our favorite Norwegian might fear that he could turn into a Swede, since not until he came to live in the U.S. did he find that he had seventy-eight Swedish relatives, all of whom invited him to their family reunion.

It's been interesting to see that the Northfield Public Library hasn't bowed down completely to our great Norwegian lovers. They didn't buy Karl Ove Knauasgaard's *My Struggle,* already predicted to win the Nobel someday. St. Olaf will save you all. They not only have his book in English but the library is happily drowning in his work in Norwegian. It's remained a library with a heart.

We shudder in remembering that in 1941 *Life* magazine helped its readers distinguish between Japanese and Chinese, using measurements by millimeters. We wished we could tell the difference between Swedes and Norwegians and even the Danish. They all looked beautiful to us, but so much alike. Sometimes you could make a guess with names. Many Danish names ended with *sen.* Norwegian names did as well, but some of them sneaked into the son "sounds" of Swedes, whereas European Swedes kept their two s's as in *sson.* Sometimes you can guess correctly if it makes any difference, but all their names derived from nature are indistinguishable. And now you might be able to spot many Scandinavians by fragrance alone. To celebrate the Viking past of York in England, its tourism agency introduced Norse Power, a body spray whose "fearsome musk" conjures the scent of those bearded tenth century conquerors. "It's hard to resist a man who smells of fresh pine, sweat, smoke, red meat, with a dash of hard liquor." Sometimes it seemed as if everyone was forgetting Iceland. Everyone except Dagmar Skulason Tisdale. Proud of her heritage, when she visited Northfield's beautiful Scandinavian store (now replaced by the equally lovely Sketchy Artist), looked around, and reminded the staff that there was nothing, no, absolutely nothing, on Iceland. Well, at least have Northfield's Iris Lee, who used to bring Icelandic fish to everyone. And there was the Paper Petulum as well, with no Icelandic flag. As for the Danish, they can also feel left out: academics in Copenhagen claim to have discovered a pattern at Ikea whereby high-end items — chairs, beds, home furnishings get named after Swedish, Finnish and Norwegian towns whereas the doormats and runners were named after Danish towns. Denmark was fed up with being treated like a doormat by the Swedish furniture giant Ikea — and being named for them too.

Who knew, that at one time that Northfielders didn't want to be Norwegian? And wasn't that Um! Yah! Yah! at St. Olaf a famous Norwegian scream? We checked out its history, and, thanks to the very knowledgable Professor David Wee, we learned that the title of the St. Olaf fight song began with an old St.Olaf faculty hymn:

> We teach at St. Olaf.
> It's built on a big bluff.
> The wind blows so hard that it causes distress.
> But colleagues are glorious,
> And students uproarious,
> There's no place on earth that we'd rather PROFESS

(This was followed by refrains made up of faculty members' names)

> Gulbrandson, Narveson, Huggenvik, Ellingson,
> Amundson, Klaragard, Halvorson, Roe.
> Fredrickson, Rasmussen, Tollefsrud, Peterson
> Skogerboe, Failletaz, Jorgenson, Boe.

(That Failletaz thingie reminds us of Sesame Street's "One of these things is not like the other). It goes on, and the names are too irresistible to leave out:

> Christensen, Sheveland, Gustafson, Maakestad,
> Lokesngaard, Skurdalsvold, Wrigglesworth, Ross.
> Rovelstad, Jacobson, Lutterman, Otterness,
> Erickson, Gunderson, Iverson, Foss.

> Thormodsgard, Bieberdorf, Overby, Gimmestad,
> Kittelsby, Ytterboe, Hinderlie, Njus.
> Ditmanson, Odegaard, Hilleboe, Anderson,
> Anderson, Anderson, Anderson, Muus!

Since no one could ever remember all these great names, "Um! Yah! Yah!" finally took its place. Kris Rosdahl Ehresmann, class of 1984, said that having Um Yah Yah is like having a secret handshake. And, it might have been David Wee who also pointed out that since it was unusual in its three quarter time or waltz meter it was possible to dance to it.

But think about the Faculty Hymn. Yes, colleagues were glorious. What other faculty ever had its own hymn? St. Olaf is the school with heart. Check out all the faculty pictures scattered around the library and all the house names as you get closer to St. Olaf on its eponymous avenue. Sing that song yourself with all those great historic names. Then think that they were all put in a blender and what came out was Um! Yah! Yah! Oh, no, we were wrong, led astray by the too-clever Professor David Wee. He made the whole thing up and given our immense respect for him, we fell for it! It's so much fun to be fooled! However, David's song lives, and St. Olaf alums at their 50th reunion loves singing it, still honoring those historic names.

OUR HIGH SCHOOL

It you weren't Norwegian it often took a long time to find yourself and find a major at St. Olaf, but Northfield High School graduates seemed to be the only people who knew what they wanted to do in life. Anyone could be anyone in the www.world. We cherished their dreams and their enticing dreaminess, grateful that they had escaped being diagnosed as having sluggish cognitive tempo. Such plans they had! They wanted to call their garage band Jackson Bryce. Samuel Hansen wanted to climb mountains in Washington State. Charles Bolstrom wanted to attend Winona State and then go to helicopter school. Zoë Henson planned to attend USC, with hopes to travel to all the continents of the world. Ryan Malecha was going to attend MCTC for Air Traffic Control. Nathan Scofield wanted to play Junior Hockey, then go to college for Chemical Engineering. Cameron Strike was going into the Air National Guard and then the University of Minnesota, Duluth. Dylan James Warner was going to a college with interest in Aviation but still continue to race at Elko Speedway. Hannah Sue Williams would attend Laramie County Community College for Early Childhood Education. The Deavonic trio, the triple threat Davis, Desiree, and Devon, were heading for St. Johns and the College of St. Benedict. Abe Cooper was going to the University of Chicago for linguistics and humanities. And

CARLETON SECURITY BLOTTER, October 31. At 11:20 pm, some students got into a fist-fight over the likeness of a dead German poet. The poet was not injured.

from Arcadia, Adele Caille plans to study Social Sciences and work with people. Gwendolyne Pietsch plans a double major in Interior Designs and Anthropology at UW-Stout. And from Randolph High, Ana Thao plans to be a marriage counselor. Adam Busch would join the Marine Corps and had enlisted while still a high school senior, then plans to serve in the infantry, and after that eventually earn a bachelor's degree in business and perhaps earn a law degree after, with the hope of opening his own bar or gym after he retires from the service.

Did any of them know how beautiful they were?

We did. In the year 2013, when three members of the NHS class of 2011 died tragically, Principal Joel Leer remembered that they had not been strangers: "These kids graduate, and they grow up and become adults and start families. But there's a certain part of development that stops when they walk across the stage at graduation, and they always stay that age for us. We remember where they sat in the lunchroom or in our class. We remember what position they played on a certain team. You build those bonds and, when something tragic happens like what happened here recently, it just punches you in the gut."

Later, the class of 2013 and many others held a memorial for their loved ones, giving their healing words NORTHFIELD STRONG, with the hope that these words can be used in many places for many events.

We often put our foot out and tried to trip these Northfield children on their march to full adulthood. But they had to leave us. They'd come back a few years later for a victory lap. And after that, they might send photos of food they enjoyed in restaurants.

OLES, CARLS, AND SOMETIMES CVECS

At least the college kids were here forever, and the colleges seemed to maintain that by never giving them a vacation but something they called a "break" in winter, spring and summer. The summers without them were lonely, except for the few who stayed to play house with premarital cooking. We missed watching them walking down the street in their ironic t-shirts with their Nalgenes. (Our favorite t-shirt said: "Irony is Non-wrinkly," but we also liked the one with a picture of Freud, that said: "Your mother's hot.") However, do you remember how hard it was to help babies give up the bottle? Well, they were all at it again—gulping water, as if no progress had been made. Still, we shared their goal of hydration and clear urine.

NORTHFIELD WOMEN OF THE RETIRED PERSUASION

Later friends began to disappear—along with their cellphone numbers. But then other friends disappeared too. White was definitely the new gray. We'd see all those white-haired women in Northfield, and think—we know them, they're our friends. People with white hair, like red cars, tended to park together. But, alas, some of them had disappeared behind a bottle of "Nice and Easy."

There were lots of disappearances through the years—when all of us of the feminine persuasion with two names, first and last, had to pick up three names and get lost to humanity. And then our names in those alumni books sounded triply boring before we were smart enough to keep our own names. People don't like triple names, even in the White House, where before admitting, they question any female with three, making one exception for Hilary Rodham Clinton. However, three names had a purpose—like Melissa Flynn Hager's name, not muffled, but still shouting: "I'm Irish."

And you've probably been emailing for years. A few tips here. LOL does not mean Lots of Love. LOL was first documented in the Oxford English Dictionary in March 2011.[16]

Accidental Aristocrats write "Cheers" at the end of their message, and it can make you feel buoyant. People of the Church sometimes write Blessings and you can feel warmed. Affectionate Aristocrats sometimes write "hugs." Hillary Clinton brought a new meaning to hugs, after she criticized Obama by planning to "hug it out" with him at a party in Martha's Vineyard. Now with "hugs" digital or real, you may be helpful to the Chinese. They're teaching it in China, and you can help American Chinese who might have missed it, with a surprise giant hug. In Nanjing, the third graders' homework was to hug their parents. Sixty schools in the district had emotional intelligence classes, according to the newspaper.

RESPECTABLE DOWNSIZING: PARTIAL AND TOTAL

Our days are numbered, we people who were here before you. We hadn't thought too too much about it until the *Northfield News* advertised deaths on the bottom of their first page. The credits were rolling. Our circle kept getting more inner. Some of us thought that at least we should accept downsizing until we came across William James, who warned that partial conversion of the loss of possessions gives a sense of the shrinking of personality, of ourselves to nothingness, and then people started talking about b----t lists, (such an ugly word, so not written out) but we knew we should hustle up. Marge and all her friends decided on theirs, cleaned the mudroom (1), and sorted their clothes by color (2). Loretta began staging her garage and then her living room, doing her best, trying to pretend she didn't live there.

As it got closer the idea of death became gentler. But why do people say, after a good dessert—"I feel like I died and went to heaven." Or that some food is to "die for?" It's quite upsetting. Is that their real preference? We didn't think too much about eternal life, or rising from the dead, until we went to an estate sale and spied the owner of the estate still in the kitchen. No one died anymore. They passed away. Then they took "away" away, and they simply passed. We got our obituary pix taken at Walgreens. It was just double duty, and the word passport seemed only right. One toasting with a wine glass seemed like fun.

But sometimes better than funerals were those memorials to Northfielders while they were alive. When Bob Stangler, son of one of Northfield's favorite pharmacists, owned the Ole Store Cafe they honored some of their neighbors with plaques on their favorite booths. There was one for Dick and Eileen Fehner, one for Charles and Lorraine Lunder, and another for Casey Jarchow. Casey's booth was frequently occupied by Doris, who knew the booth was also designed for her. Charles and Lorraine, long time customers, felt honored with the recognition, but

POLICE LOG, November 14. Suspicious person. A resident in the 5100 block of Oak Point Drive SE reported a suspicious man in the neighborhood. Police advised the resident that the man was representing the Republican Party and was speaking with local residents.

received it with humility, more accustomed to giving, not receiving. When Bob and Susan owned the cafe, they served many celebrities and the restaurant became a hideaway for college presidents; B2 was reserved for President Steven Lewis. More than other restaurants, the Ole Store reflected Northfield's changes through the years. Sandra, who had been a St. Olaf student and a waitress there knew some of its colorful history, introducing her story noting that: "You know you are in Northfield at the Ole Store when you walk into the kitchen on a busy Sunday morning and all the cooks and the dishwasher are whistling the theme to Masterpiece Theater." The Ole Store had been the West Side's grocery store. You could call in your order and they would pack it up and deliver it. There was a sauna in the 1960s in the way back and when you were done with the sauna you jumped in the cold water in the clawfoot bathtub. Modest Ole women wore bathing suits, and we don't know about everyone else. There was a cold storage locker, a walk-in cooler with numbered baskets. You would have your number, take a basket, and you could put your food in there, and you never needed your own freezer. OJ Lien who was the butcher would take all the bones and feed them to the neighborhood dogs. He always wore a white shirt and a tie under his white butcher's apron. There were a number of owners through the years. When Dale Hinderaker bought it he spent several months perfecting the Ole Roll so it would be authentic. Dale was fortunate to find a woman who rosemalled all the archways, and the place became even more Norwegian, to include nearby parking places saved For Norwegians Only. The ever-lovable Aggie kept it that way, and when she commandeered the place she never spent a day there without wearing high heels, and it is said that when she retired and began work at the Northfield Retirement Center coffee shop, the high heels stayed on. The Ole Store was also the home of the beginnings of St. Olaf student marriages; and at times the words "Will you marry me?" were overheard by other romantic guests. The stylish Todd brought new cuisine to the place, replacing the old brown booths with beautiful birchwood, fashionably uni-

I am so Northfield I remember going to retrieve frozen items for my mother from the meat locker my parents rented for what I am sure was a nominal sum from Mr. Lien at the Ole Store. — Lisa Dittman

formed St. Olaf students to the wait staff and high style dining. Later, although the furniture changed, gourmet cuisine continued to replace Scandinavian specialties, predicting a destination restaurant future, but in later days to come someone may go for another Scandinavian revival, watching that cute Norwegian Andras Vistad who celebrates the cuisine by cooking outdoors on PBS, or visit Noma in Copenhagen, now one of the world's best restaurants.

But back to honoring those who were still alive. There had been a Bridge Square ceremony for Bob Jacobsen, with a crowd much larger than a summer community concert. One special sighting at that event was a mystery man on the fringe of the crowd, dressed like an overgrown prep school boy in a summer suit and a bow tie. We found out later that he was the President of St. Olaf. There was the Purple Party for Maggie Lee at the Historical Society, where Maggie looked like royalty in her antique settee. Her song ended with "In your deep purple gown, you are everywhere in town." Our favorite memorials were the ones for Betsy Busa and her husband Romulus. Betsy's was at the St. Olaf library, a little plaque saying

In Honor of
BETSY BUSA
"The Library Mom"
July 2007

Betsy was not only the Library Mom but had also been the Library Daughter since her mother Muriel had worked in the reserve section, remembered for her light blue suit and her stories about her daughter in the Peace Corps in the Phillippines. Betsy's plaque was right under the giant plaques in honor of three St. Olaf heroes:

Harold Ditmanson   Ole E. Rolvaag   Ole G. Felland

Betsy Busa

It's only right that the Library Mom is there with all the St. Olaf Dads. Oh, now the library has taken those Dads away! At least Betsy is safe.

Not to be outdone with honoring, Carleton has inscribed a bench outside Sayles Hill to the husband of the Library Mom:

In Honor of
Romulus D. "Molly" Busa

And for those no longer with us, there were other benches to be dedicated and trees and groves of trees (for Groves Grove) for Andrea Grove Isemnger's parents. It was tempting to make a Northfield forest with each tree honoring one of us. Near Memorial Day, St. Olaf volunteers gently placed yellow chrysanthemum on each of more than 200 gravesites of deceased St. Olaf College faculty and staff buried in Northfield. It's a St. Olaf tradition that dates back more than four decades. The oldest sites date back to the 1800s.

Tim and Sue Lloyd restored a cemetery in Prairieville, east of Faribault, after a shocking but serendipitous discovery while exploring their own family genealogies on Ancestry.com. The Lloyds had moved to Northfield from Ohio, aware of no historical connections to Minnesota, but were amazed to learn that Tim's great-great-great grandfather was buried not too far from their Northfield home: on the north side of Highway 60 just past Eaton Avenue. As Sue reported to the *Northfield News*: "For more than 127 years Isaac Barrick waited for his grave to be found in a thicket of trees about two miles east of Faribault." The Prairieville Cemetery had been abandoned in the 1920s, and Isaac, born in 1793 in Maryland, moved to Cannon City Township in 1850 where he worked as a wheelwright and farmer.

The Lloyds were helped by the talented Peggy Kelly, their next-door neighbor, for whom genealogy was not only her special interest but who was also endowed with great skill at "digging" for buried headstones. Many stones were found, uncovered and mounted, but with Peggy's discovery of "Little Hervy," a lamb-shaped stone that turned out to be Isaac's grandson, the search for Isaac stepped up. Kelly refused to rest until the area was completely searched, and finally found Isaac after eight years of searching.

Tim and Sue formed an association to restore and maintain the cemetery, knowing that others waiting in the cemetery must also have relatives, and held their first Memorial Day celebration eight years ago, when only a few graves had been found and they were still killing weeds and planting grass. They wrote down the names of all the veterans in

---

POLICE LOG, November 15. Found property. A woman in the 3100 block of NW Linden Circle wanted to report that her mother found a boat on her property.

their families, bought flowers for the graves of Civil War veterans whose graves had never been buried. Peggy read the names of family members who had been in various wars, and Steve Lloyd played taps. They were the only ones there, quite a contrast to the commemorative service with a full program and eighty people in attendance when the cemetery was nearly completed. Sue wrote: "Just what will happen to the cemetery when we and the Kellys can no longer maintain it is a question many ask. We shrug our shoulders and say that we have come this far on faith, and can only hope that others will maintain it so that generations to come will have tangible evidence of the pioneers who established a town and a resting place for their family members."

We were comforted that many of our friends were still there in cyberspace. Sometimes we'd go to Google to see what was up with them and their friends who remembered. Already, we were ghosts on our Facebook page, although Google kept bullying us to change it. Funerals became a celebration (of life, that is.) Sometimes we wished for funeral choreographers, who could map the seats where everyone might sit together—family first, closest friends, the neighborhood, doctors and nurses, hospice, office colleagues, with heavy criers in the back (Kleenex rows) and then people who had just read about it in the paper. There were certain great funerals when people like the Frame family walked in, and a whole middle section of the UCC filled up.

And finally people were able to do it their way. When Jim died, it was in the midst of a blizzard and the Cremation Society couldn't get down to Northfield for five or six hours. His family decided to have a ceremony and when the doctor called and asked "What can I do?" the answer was "Go get wine and food." Jim had many happy trails after that. His kids took some of his ashes to Boulder and some to Bozeman. He (and his) also went to the Statue of Jeanne d'Arc in Paris and Giverny. He went to his cottage in Iowa, to his rose garden at home, and his metal-detecting buddies took him back to the field in England where they had detected for years. They took pictures of themselves all lined up holding their detectors, and after Jim's ashes were dropped, they followed up with a final shot with one detector standing alone without an owner.

And then there were the beloved ones all over in the sky. After Judith had given a star away to her father when he died, she knew that she got to see him every night. Her friend, in turn, missing her husband terribly, at first gave him a star and then decided it would be more effective to give him the moon, so large and easy to locate. "He also gets exceptional dawns and sunsets. Don't let the folks at observatory know that he owns quite a bit of the galaxy."

We wanted all of our Northfielders to stay alive in our memories, and sometimes their obituaries didn't do it; some, but not all, seemed to have been written by the funeral director reading a questionnaire. We think it would be great if we started practicing writing our own obituaries, with a few blank pages for our great loved ones to write so they won't feel left out. Who knows you better than you? Who has a better sense of your own comic part in the human comedy? Who dares speak of your own life struggles? It may be your only chance for a biography or at least a final farewell, sharing your wisdom. If you do it in 20,000 words, you reach celebrity status and save your local newspaper from bankruptcy for a month. John Paul II, with the longest, came in at 13,363 words. Go for it. YODO. You only die once.

Northfield needed something special. The L & M Bar with free beer for breakfast attracted Jay Leno, and Garrison Keillor read from the *Northfield News*, once famous for their Police Log (the remnants of which you can find scattered here). But what have they got now? If we all did our own writing, we could have colorful obituaries, writing about our real selves. And then everyone in Northfield could celebrate not only the defeat of the James gang, but have a celebration for Obituary Days, with Victorian ladies walking up and down Division Street in black with a few veils hiding their faces, and men in old-fashioned suits with black armbands. Probably the Jesse James costume shop could contribute. There would be a special reading of the Obituaries of the Year, with a Loving Cup to the survivors of the best life story.

On that first morning after Northfield was named the second best small city in the nation, those who had grown up here (and some who hadn't) took their last Ole Roll out of the freezer, dipped their own home-made madeleine in milk and coffee and thought about us, and their lives here. What was thus palpitating in the depths of their being was the image, the visual memory which, being linked to that taste, they tried to follow into their conscious mind. Immediately they remembered the stage set they could see looking down Third Street—the Sketchy Artist, Anna's Closet, the Center for the Arts. And an exquisite pleasure invaded their senses. They knew that somewhere deep inside, they still belonged to Northfield, although a fossilized Northfield, and they wrote:

Andy: I'm so Northfield, I think being #2 is just fine

David Flanagan: I'm so Northfield that I gotta say: Darnit, why didn't Northfield have its own nuclear reactor?

Lora: My friends I've made there, they're so Northfield that they know how to be real and true friends, and the concept of "fair weather friend" doesn't even exist in their vocabulary.

Chris: I'm so Northfield when I heard about the "stress positions" used for torture at Guantanamo, all I could think of was junior high gym class with Berkvam and Dommeyer.

T. McKinley: I'm now so Northfield I feel like the top of my head has floated away and I finally have room to think, to imagine and wonder.

I'm so Northfield I had to write another book about it.

Love, Nancy

POLICE LOG, November 21. Officers were called when a male was found at the library sitting on top of a building holding a rifle and a rose. Upon arrival, officers learned that the individual was taking senior pictures with a paintball gun.

ACKNOWLEDGEMENTS

I put things together, but you did the rest, especially those who took an early interest in the book, so here's to you Mirjana Urosev, the divine Ms M from Santa Monica, who fell so in love with Northfield after reading *Fantasy Northfield*, that she offered us family vacations in her parents' houses in Detroit. Only Mirjana was allowed to see whole pages of this book in advance, and we'll always have Detroit.

And here's to my family: the exciting new additions, Kate Wheeler, Dylan, Ellie and Owen, who joined Chris Soth, Andy Soth, Lauren Soth (yay), Amelia, Lucy & Madison Soth, Ruth Flanagan, David Flanagan the Bamboo Fencer, and Carolyn Cox Flanagan. And here's to the Fishwives, the Drinking Grannies, and the Trophy Wives.

Thanks to the Literary Giants who wrote huge sections of the book, some of whom later gave me permission to steal: T McKinley, Elizabeth O'Sullivan, Sandra, Marie Gery, Lydia Quanbeck Moe, Barbara Clark, Jan Roberts, Helen Preddy, Karen and David Wee, Kiffi Summa, Leslie Schultz, Martha Davies, Molly Woehrlin, Susan Lloyd, and Susan Hvistendahl, that talented journalist from the journalism empire. And, Arthur Paul David White, of course. (I remember looking into his penetrating innocent blue eyes before the last book I wrote, telling him what I had written and hoping he'd forgive me. Now I am hoping for lifetime assurance.)

Here's to Jim Fisher, who gave *Fantasy Northfield* to the incoming, history-loving President Robert Oden, who quoted passages from it in his inaugural address. Moreover, for many years, Jim opened every conversation with greetings that book recommended: "Love Your Hair."

Here's to Kristine Holmgren who told us about Northfield poet Kai Carlson-Wee. Who even knew that any Carlsons had teamed up with any Wees?

Many names are used in this book. They often gave permission. If they didn't, or I didn't ask for it, their names remain here as Innocent Bystanders. In this acknowledgement, I want to concentrate on those who might be surprised that they are here, apologize if I must, and you might want to let them know they reside herein. This includes the Northfield graduates who had already planned their lives, and the Northfield High

School young artists, and Principal Joel Leer. And there are the Pretend Husbands, whom you can read about, as well as the veterans. Thanks to all those who told me about their churches or their spiritual lives: Ann Knutson, Marge Tarr, Al Gramstedt, Julie, Julia Braulick, Zach Thompson, Gary Gleason, Larry Cooper, Betsy Lane-Getz, Sam Demas, Laura Kay Allen, Corinne Smith, Norm Vig and Carol Oliver, Pastor Daniel Runke, Rev. Kristin Maier, Rev. Gayle Marsh, and poet Padre Spencer Reece, mentioned only because it feels good to know a Padre. And there was Father Denny. So impressed and moved to receive invitations to special church events by the Spanish-speaking community at St. Dominic, I asked him to write about how he helped to make it possible. You may be assured that this is not the only wonderful celebration or service at St. Dominic, but since we no longer have Cinco de Mayo on Bridge Square, it seemed important. Having Father Denny contribute to this book made me want to be careful that it was without bad language or thoughts or overloaded satire. I approached Griff Wigley, who had given me permission to copy a few choice passages from Locally Grown, which I always thought of as the Green Network, about my desire to protect, who assured me that he had gone to seminary with Father Denny, (although he hadn't followed in his footsteps.) I am not sure that makes me feel safe, but it was Northfield news I'd love to use. As to other churches, when a bystander did not arise, there was good information from the church websites.

And thanks to Mark Heiman, brilliance itself, an editor, masked as a publisher, who could turn stream of consciousness into almost immediate organization, even a guidebook. It was if God had a better view and could look down on and fix a messy Earth.

My Favorite Innocent Bystander was the then Third Grader, Hannah Farmer, who wrote: "MY CARE. My parents are who I care about. No person can replace them, not even a mouse." I must find her, and I think she might be in Duluth. There's the sidewalk poet, whose name I just learned: Lilly Hanlon, who on the library hill provided a good technique for writing a book or even a poem. There are the remarkable brothers,

POLICE LOG, November 23. Someone was reported to have picked up the Safety Center dispatch phone and said "You are a slave."

surely their parents' pride: Abraham, Emmanuel, Gabriel, and Isaiah Suarez. Joey and Edward Enders, Astrid White, Zoë and Celeste Jarman, Jill Ewald, Peggy Kelly. Dale Touchette, Leota Goodney, Jan Stevens, Beth Schott, Guy Reid, Karen Oiseth, Linda Stadler, Jean Larson, Senora Barrientos, Joan Wolf Bundy, Penny Bond, Joan Reitz, David Peterson, Toni Easterson, Kirsten Johnson, Jan Shoger, Betsy Busa, Pat Winter, Wendell Arneson, Nancy Carlson, Susan Crow, Sue Hammes-Knopf, Mary Rose, Loren Larson, Megan Wille, Cindy, the ER nurse whose last name I've forgotten, Felicity Enders, Doug Bratland, Shouri Daniels, Rick Louis, Jim McCorkell, Victor Summa, Dr. Mark Mellstrom, Helen Woehrlin, Laurie Pankow, Judy De Long, Dr. William Saul, David Peterson, Sam Harris, Gene Enders, Peg Enders, Dr. Ed Lufkin (in disguise), Rick Swearer, Diane Angell, Kofi Owusu, Dr. Gretchen Ehresmann, Maumoune Toure-Keita, Jane McDonnell, Nancy Pelosi, Terri Quamme, Bereket Haileab, Governor Dayton, Lindy Morral, Ann Wright, Charlotte Smith, Leah Daniels, Iris Lee, Krittika Ramanujan, Ruth Weiner, Judith Mason, Ed Sostek, Sarah Bardenwerper, Lucy, Ann & Easton Archibald, David Wellstone, Kathleen Flynn, Ruth Flanagan, Russ Langworthy, the Sullivans (Dan & Ann), the Lavenders (Val & David), John Perry, Marion Anderson, Pope Francis, Cherif Keita, Bill Child, Kitty Runzheimer, Thad Caron, Jenna Kuhlman, Dan Dressen, John Fossum, Ruth Legvold, Melissa Hager, Paul Auster, Siri Hustvedt, Esther Hustvedt, Leah Wellstone, Stephen Mohring, Mary, Mallory & Alison Easter, Leona Openshaw, Gloria Steinem, Lois Lowry, Elizabeth Schott, John Schott, Claude O'Neill, Peggy Prowe, Anne Ulmer, Nikki Lamberty, Olena Fimyar, LaVern Rippley, Rodney King, Alice Thomas, Lucy Sweitzer, Mac Gimse, Raphael Estrella, Christie Clark, Myrna Johnson, Dan Kallman, Andrea Grove Iseminger, Katherine Noorhis, the Sketchy Artist, April Ripka, Deb Supps, Helen Dillon, Eileen Seeley, Charlotte Brackee, Laurie Brackee, Bri Seeley, Frances Crouter, Julia Bly, Olivia Fantini, Keith Harrison, Romulus Busa, Glynnis Lessing, Suzanne Riesman, Charlie Cogan and Raphaela, Marian Tuma, Pat Trcka, Jerry Mohrig, John Benjamin, Deane Barbour, Barbara Smith Hill, Jonathan Hill, Alex Robins, Ross Shoger, Susan Cain, Jo Zimmerman, Andrea Een, Loris Damerow, Corinne Heiberg, Marion Hvistendahl, Bart and Sue deMalignon, Susan Bauer, Jane Greenwood, Jim McDonnell, Kristi Casson, Susan Toth

Eggener, Mary Jo Oberling, Dagmar Tisdale, Carole Christensen, Jean Wakely, Krin Finger, Dale Finger, the Estrems, Kaj Fjelstad, Vanessa Bodrie, Addie Rosenwinkel, Marlis Schmid, Randy Malecha, Norman Butler, Diane Burry, Kevin Willie, Annette Wagner, Rosella Cullen, Ed Klinkhammer, Ruth & Doug Crane, Will Healy, Christina Harrison, Larry Anthony, Frederick Kettering, Billi Bergh, Nancy Cantwell, Katrina Harrison, Krishna Ramanujan, Kris Rosdahl Ehresmann, Amelia, Lucy, and Madison.

POLICE LOG. *Sudden Death. Sometime after November, sometime around 2007, the most popular representation of Northfield's Finest as well as Northfield's finest journalism disappeared without reason, without investigation, explanation or the help of detectives. HELP.*

www.ingramcontent.com/pod-product-compliance
Lightning Source LLC
LaVergne TN
LVHW051352080426
835509LV00020BB/3400